MIRACLE *in the* DESERT

MIRACLE *in the* DESERT

A JOURNEY OF SELF-DISCOVERY AFTER A STROKE

Authored By,

Marco Giovannoli

Disclaimer

Registered Office- 907-Sneh Nagar, Sapna Sangeeta Road,
Agrasen Square, Indore – 452001 (M.P.), India

Website: http://www.wingspublication.com

Email: mybook@wingspublication.com

First Published by WINGS PUBLICATION 2023

Title : Miracle in the Desert

ISBN : 978-81-19223-88-6

LIMITS OF LIABILITY/DISCLAIMER OF WARRANTY

Dedication

I dedicate this book to all those who have supported me on my journey with a stroke and continue to do so each day. Your love, encouragement, and belief in my strength have been my guiding light. This dedication is a tribute to the profound impact you've each had on my life. Thank you for standing by me, lifting me up, and being my rock.

A special dedication to my son, Gabriele. I wish you all the best, and I'm committed to being a significant part of your life.

Similarly, this is dedicated to all the medical staff I encountered since my stroke, especially at NMC ProVita, whose expertise helped me regain most of my lost functionalities after the stroke. I am grateful for their ongoing support in helping me get better and alleviating the consequences of this challenging journey. This book is for stroke survivors, and anyone involved with them.

To Lei, Metha, and my mum—your solid belief in my writing abilities fueled me as I embarked on this book journey.

For Lei, the steady presence that holds my hand through the post-stroke journey. With you, I am never alone.

To my incredible team members and colleagues, your solid support and seamless acceptance of my return, as if nothing had happened, have been my driving force. Your willingness to alleviate work stress from my shoulders daily has granted me the space to focus on my journey. This bond is irreplaceable, and I would not trade it for anything else.

I would also like to express my gratitude for my stroke. It brought me challenges, but it also became the catalyst for discovering my new self and purposes in life. It granted me the opportunity to embark on the remarkable journey of writing this book. I am thankful for the lessons learned and the transformation it sparked within me.

Contents

Premise

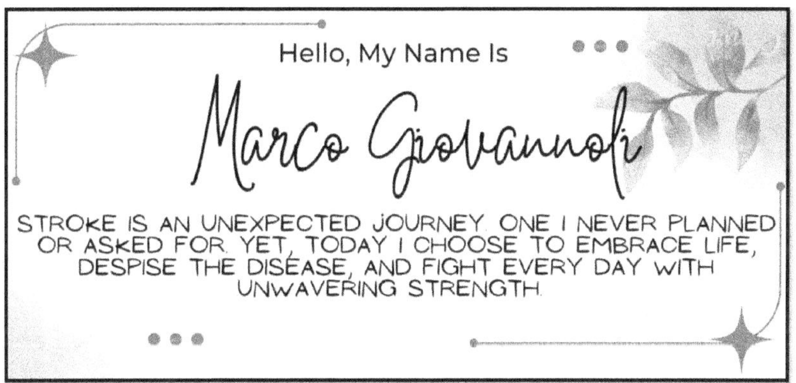
Hello, My Name Is
Marco Giovannoli
STROKE IS AN UNEXPECTED JOURNEY. ONE I NEVER PLANNED OR ASKED FOR. YET, TODAY I CHOOSE TO EMBRACE LIFE, DESPISE THE DISEASE, AND FIGHT EVERY DAY WITH UNWAVERING STRENGTH.

Foreword

Disclaimer: The original message has been reviewed and corrected for grammatical accuracy.

Dear Marco,

The credit solely goes to you.

We have discussed this concept before, and I want to remind you that every condition is approached biologically, psychologically, and sociologically. This comprehensive approach is known as the biopsychosocial model.

In many cases, individuals affected by stroke or other physical disabilities do not experience complete recovery; they might recover biologically (physically) but not psychologically, or they might recover both biologically and psychologically but not sociologically.

You stand out from other patients in this regard. You have achieved recovery in all three dimensions. Your openness, self-perseverance, motivation, and hard work have played a significant role. You grasped the essence of our discussions, understanding the importance of both short-term and long-term goals, the value of self-motivation, and the tremendous support from your family, girlfriend, and co-workers. They have collectively helped you build psychological and sociological resilience.

Your willingness to go to the office, engage in outside activities, volunteer to assist other stroke survivors, create motivational TikTok videos, and continue with your regular routines without hesitation demonstrates your unique strength. You are harnessing every potential you possess.

Keep up the fantastic work, Mr. Marco. Stay motivated and keep inspiring others. Remain happy and healthy.

Metha Gowsic V

Physical Therapist at NMC ProVita

Preface

> "There's no such thing as coincidence, I say. It's synchronicity."
>
> RAVEN KALDERA

"It is an amazing idea; I have always dreamt of writing a book!" I answered Lei when she suggested that I author a book about my journey with the stroke.

Metha, my therapist at NMC ProVita, told me one morning while we were walking back to my room, "You should write a book about your journey to inspire others. I see too many patients who just give up on therapy and life. They close themselves off and behave like children."

Building on Ian Fleming's: "Once is happenstance. Twice is coincidence. Three times is enemy action," I say, "One occurrence is luck, two occurrences are a coincidence, but three occurrences establish a pattern."

My third push came when I received a call from my mum just a couple of weeks after I had started drafting this book. During one of our daily conversation, she mentioned an article in the Italian newspaper about a radio presenter who had suffered a stroke and published a book about her adventure. Thus, she encouraged me to do the same.

While I have learned from doing statistics and data analysis on my job that 'correlation doesn't imply causation,' I do believe that these occurrences were not mere coincidences but rather synchronicities. They were messages to me. Synchronicities hold deeper significance and remind us that there is a greater plan at play in our lives.

The psychotherapist Jung chose the term synchronicity to explain the occurrence of events happening at the same time. It seems to have no obvious cause but holds significant meaning. The word combines "syn," meaning "with," and "chronos," meaning "time."

While some may argue that coincidences are random, upon closer examination of our lives, we come to realize that they are not. Every word we hear, every sound that reaches our ears, and every person we meet are not mere chance encounters. They come into our lives precisely when we need them the most, offering answers to our inner doubts and questions. These seemingly serendipitous moments hold deeper meaning and purpose. They guide us along our journey, providing the support and insights we seek.

Serendipity is when something unexpected and good happens by chance. It is like stumbling upon a hidden treasure or finding a solution to a problem without even trying. Serendipity is all about pleasant surprises that make life more interesting and exciting.

Conversely, synchronicity is the guide when we find ourselves uncertain about which path to choose or what changes to make in our lives. It is as if someone, somewhere above, hears our silent prayers and communicates with us through other individuals, images, or events. In fact, Einstein described coincidences as being "God's way of remaining unknown," highlighting their mysterious and profound nature. These synchronistic experiences offer us insights and messages from the universe. They provide a sense of divine guidance. They remind us that there is something greater at work in our lives. Of course, the list of synchronicities can be endless and subjective as synchronicity is a more complex phenomenon. However, Albert Einstein says, "There is no logical way to the discovery of these elemental laws. There is only the way of intuition, which is helped by a feeling for the order lying behind the appearance."

It was a crisp sunny morning like many others in Abu Dhabi. I was seated still on my couch, and I was in a good sweat after my stroke rehabilitation routine 45 minutes morning walk although I had already had a refreshing shower and one good Italian coffee to recharge my batteries.

A bright ray of sunlight fell upon me through the living room window, mingling with the cool stream emanating from the centralized air-cooling system. This collision of warm and cold fronts near my skin resembled a pocket-size tornado. Meanwhile, my left hand gracefully danced across the page, breathing life into the story you hold in your hands.

I was pressing my lips together while I cast my mind back to my days in primary school. I found myself reminiscing about the experience of reading my compositions aloud in front of classes as a form of reward for my effort.

Without warning, I was transported back to those days. Reading in front of a class was a daunting task, evoking a wave of anxiety that surged through every fiber of my being.

As I stand before my peers, their expectant eyes fixated on me, a sense of self-consciousness creeps in. The weight of their judgment feels palpable, intensifying the nervousness coursing through my veins. My heart races like a wild stallion. The mere thought of stumbling over words or mispronouncing a passage fills me with dread. The fear of ridicule and the desire to meet expectations collide. The words on the page blur as anxiety cloud my concentration, making it difficult to even comprehend the sentences before me. With shaky hands, I grip my notebook tightly, my voice trembling as I utter the first words. Each syllable feels like a hurdle to overcome. But with each passing sentence, the anxiety gradually decreases. As the final word escapes my lips, a rush of relief washes over me. I know I have faced my fears and conquered the challenge of reading in front of a class. The memory of sharing my composition, cherished like a treasured keepsake, forever etched in my mind.

A few years later, when I was around 18 or 19 years old, I found myself lying in my bed at my parents' house, lost in a daydream. In that moment, I envisioned myself crafting a book, but I had no notion of its subject matter. Little did I know that 30 years down the road, a stroke would unlock the sleeping writer within me, held hostages for all those years, setting me free to explore the skill of storytelling.

> And by the way, everything in life is writable about if you have the outgoing guts to do it, and the imagination to improvise. The worst enemy to creativity is self-doubt.

Sylvia Plath

In the wake of my stroke, I have come to realize that every aspect of life holds a story waiting to be written. I have found courage within myself to put those thoughts and experiences into words. The stroke may have affected my physical abilities, but it has not taken away my imagination. In fact, it has pushed me to improvise and find new ways to express myself through writing. The true obstacle I face is the self-doubt that lingers in the corners of my mind. It tries to discourage me from sharing my stories, but I am determined not to let it stifle my creativity.

In life, there is always something to write about if you dare to do it and let your imagination flow freely. Doubting yourself hinders creativity, so I will push beyond those barriers. Life's experiences, both big and small, are worth putting into words, and I am ready to explore and express them with courage and imagination. There is a world of stories waiting to be told, and I will not let self-doubt stand in the way of sharing my voice with the world.

Drafting a book in a dreamscape indicates a desire to be creative. Perhaps I was in need to explore a new hobby to stretch my creative muscles, or 30 years later, I was looking for a new purpose and meaning in life after my stroke, or it was indicating a need of communication between me and someone else or me and my subconscious. Hence, I shelved that dream at the back of my mind and moved on with my life, because I thought I did not have what it takes to be a writer.

Still to this day, while I am drafting this book, I am not convinced that anything I am writing is good enough (see also: imposter syndrome). According to Robert H. Schuller, “The only place where your dream becomes impossible is in your own thinking.”

“Do you know what makes life confusing? It is when you cannot determine if things are signs for you to give up or simply a test to see if you can hold on longer” (Unknown). As much as I never really believed in signs, I do believe that events can be used to validate our thoughts and decisions (see also confirmation bias), like writing a book. Perhaps, it is the benevolent universe trying to speak to us. Ultimately, even if the universe does send us signs, how we interpret them is purely subjective and our subjectivity makes the difference on how we translate our thoughts in actions. Dr. Srikumar Rao states that the "Universe is benevolent, and it is on our side," and we should "learn to see the good in whatever comes to us."

It was 25th of April 2023, a normal working day, when my friend and one of the best, or undoubtedly the best physiotherapist I have ever met, Metha Gowsic Velayutham, sent me the following message in the middle of a discussion we were having about my stroke rehabilitation, "And u r really doing very good Marco. U r really an inspiration. You should write a book about your experience." This was not the first time Metha suggested that I had to write a book about my experience with stroke.

In addition, on the same day, my friend, Cristiano, from Sao Paolo (Brazil) told me, "We just need to listen to him (God), see the signs!" after I had told him, "I believe there is something good waiting for me." Mehta's and Cristiano's messages were the final signs I was looking for that unequivocally made it clear to me that my new purpose in life was to write this book about my recovery from a stroke to help others in my same situation.

However, the initial idea to write a book was born from Lei. I was still an in-patient at the rehabilitation center when she suggested that I write a book about my recovery.

It was a Saturday at NMC ProVita International Medical Centre Abu Dhabi (UAE's largest provider of post-acute care and rehabilitation services). A Saturday like any other for three months. The day started the way it should have. Early morning wakeup call by the birds resting outside my window. Generally, they started chirping in chorus as the sun rises, as they do, they begin to sing their different songs. All together, they sound like a boisterous cacophony, but soon you hear their individual sounds, which becomes a symphony of beauty and awe.

I had a light breakfast followed by a one-hour stationary bike workout. Subsequently, while playing chess (I was trying to learn and play chess to train my cognitive skills like memory, planning, and problem-solving), Lei articulated, "You should write a book to share your story with everyone that there is hope for recovery after a stroke if you believe it."

Thenceforth, we talked about writing this book many times to define the theme and its plot. We tried to identify the most notable events to cover in the book. She has always believed I could draft this book. Lei is my first fan and supporter on this journey. She made me accountable for typing a minimum of five hundred words per day to complete this book in a reasonable period.

Introduction

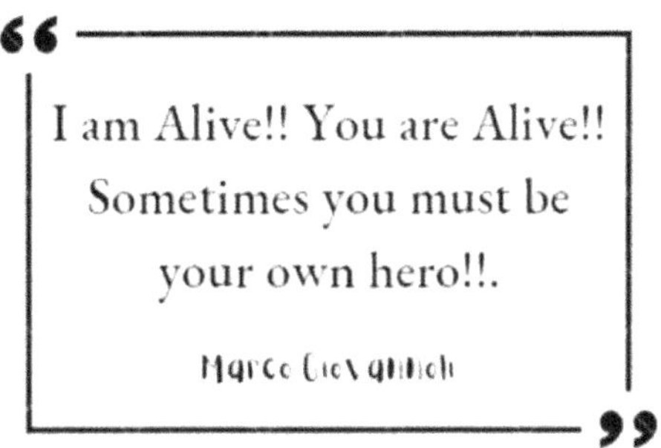

In the hot desert, a stroke struck, and darkness loomed. But a miracle happened! I started a journey to find myself. Even though it was hard, life's challenges shaped me and showed my bravery. Get ready for an amazing story of strength and discovery in the desert! This is my personal hero journey. A transformative adventure filled with challenges and growth. It reflects my own experiences, where I faced obstacles, found allies, and discovered inner strength.

Living every day with a stroke is undeniably the most challenging experience I have ever faced. The difficulties, the frustrations, and the constant adjustments are a part of my new reality that I am learning to navigate. People would often ask me how I am coping with the deficiencies that came after the stroke. They genuinely care, but finding the right words to explain the emotional and physical toll is never easy. "It's hard, It's so fuck@ing hard living every day with a stroke!!" I would reply, my voice tinged with the weight of the struggle.

Facing each day with physical limitations is an uphill battle. Tasks that were once effortless now demand tremendous effort and patience. The simplest of movements had become obstacles in themselves. There are days when I feel defeated, questioning whether I would ever regain some sense of normalcy. Staying positive is a constant challenge. The emotional rollercoaster feels never-ending. I have my moments of frustration and sadness, and I must remind myself that it is okay to feel that way. But amidst it all, I try to find glimmers of hope and small victories. Those are the sparks that keep me moving forward.

Adapting to my new reality means not just adjusting physically but also emotionally. It is essential to acknowledge my feelings and confront the emotional toll the stroke takes on me. Seeking support from friends, family, and sometimes professionals helped me navigate this unfamiliar territory. The road to healing is slow, but I am willing to give myself the time and space I need. Living with a stroke means embracing a new version of myself. It is an ongoing process of self-discovery and acceptance. Though the road is filled with obstacles, I know that with time and patience, I can find ways to overcome them.

Stroke is a leading cause of mortality and disability worldwide (Katan and Luft, 2018). The most common forms of stroke are ischemic and hemorrhagic, which account for 11.8% of deaths worldwide (Feigin et al., 2014).

My name is Marco Giovannoli. I had a stroke in September 2022. I am not going to lie to you every day, this stroke takes such a heavy toll on me, in all aspects.

Spoiler Alert: This book springs forth from my left hand alone. Once right-handed, this stroke altered my path.

It continues to try to drag me down. But I keep fighting back, pouring my energy into overcoming the obstacles that I face. I have come to accept that recovery will be an ongoing journey throughout my life. After a less-than-a-year-long recovery, I am coping quite well with my deficiencies. I am managing the challenges of fatigue, as well as muscle stiffness and tightness. There is still weakness in my right upper and lower limbs, and I experience sensory processing issues.

During moments of self-doubt and uncertainty, I find solace in repeating a mantra to myself: "I am Alive!"! You are Alive!! Sometimes you shall be your own hero!!" These words serve as a powerful reminder that I possess an inner strength and resilience that can guide me through any challenge. When faced with adversity, I draw upon the courage within me, embracing the idea that I can be my own hero. This mantra is a constant reminder to me of my inherent vitality and the endless possibilities that lie ahead.

Every time I look in the mirror and see myself, I see a living, breathing thing staring at me. That reflection is a strong reminder of the fact that I am alive.

I am grateful for being alive. I am a true miracle, a “Miracle in the Desert.” Despite all odds and all medical predictions, I survived the acute ischemic stroke I had in early September 2022. Lei, my current life companion, gave me this epithet, which also became the title of this book. The idea that I had a second chance, I would say a second life, to achieve something new and bigger gives me the strength and motivation to sit and write down my personal story as a stroke survivor. I will explain the physical, emotional, and psychological effects of stroke on me. I want to encourage others in similar conditions to embrace resilience and hope in the face of adversity.

In life, our beliefs hold the power to shape our reality. "We are what we believe we are." This profound truth reminds us that our self-perception and convictions create the foundation of our existence. Embracing positive and empowering beliefs about ourselves can lead to newfound confidence and limitless possibilities. Conversely, if we harbor self-doubt or limiting beliefs, they can hinder our growth and potential. By recognizing the influence of our beliefs, we can harness their transformative force and embark on a journey of self-discovery, allowing us to unveil the boundless potential within us.

“You will need to accept that some limitations will be with you in the future,” was the advice from my friend, Masoud, during one of our talks at the rehabilitation center. I know his intentions were good. More than a friend, he has always been a brother to me. He was trying to protect me from possible distresses and frustration if I would not get back where I wanted to be. However, it would take time for me to understand that.

For a long time, I held to the belief—or it was only a dream of mine—that things would go back to how they once were. I just needed to be discharged from the hospital and start my rehabilitation program. This conviction gave me something to focus on that felt real during a time of disruption and uncertainty. Unfortunately, reality would prove to be different to my dream.

As much as I wanted things to be like they once were, my life was taking a different path. I had to accept that ***my life would never be the same.*** Like a coin with two sides, I now had an observe side—my life before the stroke. The opposite side, now representing me after the stroke.

This acceptance was important for me to set reasonable expectations about my recovery. Patience, practice, and positivity besides acceptance, are all important aspects when working on a reliable post-stroke rehabilitation program. To avoid unpleasant surprises during your recovery, set reasonable goals. When setting realistic goals, you will need to think about the required actions to take with them. This can help you set the pace while keeping you responsible for your actions.

Do not set unachievable or arbitrary recovery goals!! You are throwing a monkey wrench into your rehab. I learned the hard way that this approach does not help to fast-track a post-stroke recovery. Within two weeks of having my stroke, I decided that I would be able to control my right hand. But after almost a year, I am still experiencing extensive muscle weakness in my right limbs. There is stiffness and tightness, known as spasticity, and loss of fine motor control in my right hand.

I have realized that physical, spiritual, and emotional health are all linked. One supporting the other. Taking care of all aspects will increase the likelihood that I will feel better in this life-long voyage.

***

On the morning of May 06, 2023, as part of my routine post-stroke rehabilitation program, I was walking along the saltwater canals close to my apartment. I always loved these morning walks where I would either listen to a podcast about self-growth and positive mindset or I would be fully absorbed in my thoughts by slowing down my brain waves to tune down the volume of the negativity and nuisance going on in my life and in my head.

I would try to contact my feelings and evaluate what is going on inside and around me to try to reach a state of peace within myself. That day, because my phone podcast application kept buffering for several minutes, I decided to drop the headset, and instead, I chose to use that two-hour walk to reflect on this same book you are reading.

I have always experienced an inner peace when walking along those canals; although my attention and the sequence of thoughts would be disturbed by the noise coming from the endless construction sites along the canals from time to time.

While walking, I recalled reading an online article about people experiencing the benefits of the water whether they are near the ocean, a lake, river, swimming pool, or even listening to the soothing sound of a fountain. Wallace Nichols, a marine biologist, and author of the 2014 book, *Blue Mind*, specifies, "Most communities are built near bodies of water not just for practical reasons, but because as humans, we're naturally drawn to blue space...but even if you aren't in an area where there is easy access to water, you can still experience [its] emotional benefits."

Walking beside the tranquil canals has become a soul-nourishing ritual, offering me a myriad of emotional benefits. As I stroll along the water's edge, the gentle lapping of the waves creates a calming rhythm that soothes my mind, washing away the stresses of daily life. The scenic beauty of the surrounding landscape immerses me in a sense of serenity, filling my heart with gratitude for nature's wonders. The unhurried pace of the canal's flow mirrors my own, allowing me to find a peaceful rhythm within. Each step offers a moment for introspection, as I find solace in solitude, fostering a deeper connection with my thoughts and emotions.

I was staring at the free-floating weed gently pulled along by the continuous flow of water and at the fish gasping for air on the surface; the canals' oxygen levels always dip to dangerously low levels when the air and water temperature upsurge during summer “and/or” because of high ammonia and nitrite/nitrate levels found in the saltwater in the part of the world that I am currently living in.

“Physical impairments are not limitations, but stimulus to find new paths and a better self in life.” These words were born in my subconscious mind, like the creation of an artesian spring when the pressure for the groundwater becomes greater than the pressure from the atmosphere and the water is pushed straight up out of the ground. In this case, words were pushed from my deep inner realm up to my conscious mind and I pondered Heraclitus’ words: “Everything flows, and nothing abides; everything gives way, and nothing stays fixed.” These words made me appreciate that we are like water; we always change, we evolve at every step and turn in our life. Now and here, we are the product of our beliefs, thoughts, and ultimately, actions. Every step shall be a step forward towards new experiences and possibly a more fulfilled life.

Heraclitus went on to add that "The only constant in life is change." That concept presents us with limitless new initiations, whether we are kicking off a new year, recovering from a loss/illness/accident, starting a new job, or jumping into a new relationship. Every day the sun rises is a new beginning, and that is a reason to be excited!

As humans, we cannot help but lean toward getting meaning and purpose in our lives. We hunt for it in the pages we read (hopefully, this book will be helpful to you in this quest), scroll endless internet pages, and browse for it in the aisles of stores.

We look for them at work and pursue them in our relationships. We are always trying to make sense of our experiences.

Accepting my current physical limitations, the emotional distress, and the consequent life challenges that the stroke gifted me, allowed me to start looking at my life from a unique perspective. Slowly—slowly—I learnt how to shift my viewpoint and develop a cheerful outlook to build a meaningful life by finding new meaning and purposes. I reframed the way I think. I forced myself to stay in the moment and live with the present as a daily gift we receive every day. The future is unknown to us and discovering it now will kill the mystery.

I have started appreciating all the small 1% gains (the principle of 'aggregate marginal gains') and progress in life along with all the nice and beautiful things life brings to my attention every day. I discovered new passions and repressed ones have risen again. This book is the outcome of my life evolution after the stroke.

Changing for the better is not an easy task. It requires patience, perseverance, dedication, and commitment toward us and the people we love and care for. We may be required to ditch old habits, to look at our life and its events in diverse ways, to embrace changes in our mind, heart, and soul. We may decide to embrace new faiths from scratch, stay centered in our current ones, or reclaim old ones.

Luckily enough, I am not the first and not the last to speak about this concept. English philosopher James Allen wrote: "As a man thinks, so he is; as he continues to think, so he remains." Stoic and Roman emperor Marcus Aurelius wrote: "A man's life is what his thoughts make of it." Poet and philosopher Ralph Waldo Emerson wrote: "A man is what he thinks about all day long." Author Earl Nightingale said: "We become what we think about," and Mark Twain wrote: "Life consists mainly of the storm of thoughts that is forever flowing through one's head."

"Never feel guilty for starting again but feel at fault for the inertia stain," I told myself while drafting this page.

This book provides a detailed chronology of the events as they have happened from the morning I suffered the stroke, and my subsequent rehabilitation journey up to now as I am typing these same words.

It is also the account of my emotional struggles of accepting my new conditions. The continuous inner work to fight negativity and the search for new purposes in my life.

At this point, you will realize that this book is not really about stroke, but more about what this stroke has taught me about myself and life in general. It covers my emotional and mental struggles trying to escape depression, which is always lurking in the shadows, waiting for the right opportunity to grab me.

The accounts I share in this book are about the love from my family and friends. How they were so important and how they are still helping me every day with my emotional and physical recovery.

This book also covers my personal experience with the medical support I received in the United Arab Emirates, which has played—and still does play—a pivotal role in my recovery. I crossed and interacted with many amazing professionals. From the Emergency Responders to the medical Teams at Sheikh Shakhbout Medical City (SSMC) and especially at NMC ProVita, who helped me physically and emotionally. I am currently here writing this book also because of them.

In writing this book, I used Hemingway's writing style, embracing the art of brevity. I employed short and simple sentences. I tried to evoke his essence, creating a narrative that resonates with succinctness and clarity. I tried to capture the power of every word. Clarity helps you to understand exactly what I am saying. Brevity keeps your attention. Both clarity and brevity are about keeping things simple and short. They are crucial in today's world filled with overwhelming amounts of information.

Ladies and gentlemen, this is your writer and aircraft pilot speaking. Welcome aboard this exciting journey as we prepare to take flight into the world of my book. Please fasten your seatbelts. Be ready to immerse yourselves in the pages ahead. Just like a thrilling flight, this book promises to take you on an adventure through captivating stories and heartfelt moments. Relax, and get ready to soar through the skies of imagination as we embark on this incredible reading journey together. Thank you for joining me. I hope you enjoy the ride! More than anything, I am grateful to be alive and celebrative of the time I have here in this world. Lastly, I am excited that these words will be spread out into the world where they might do good.

The Me
I Used to Be

"Who am I?" gets at the heart of one of our most basic needs: our need for identity.

"Who was Marco before the stroke?" This question echoed in my head so many times over the years. It is such a simple question, and at the same time, so intrinsically difficult to respond to. One of the archetypal metaphysical question along to good vs bad and power vs resistance since the appearance of a conscious humankind.

Figure 1- Marco proudly wearing an Abu Dhabi Striders t-shirt.

According to Shahram Heshmat Ph.D., author of Science of Choice, “Identity relates to our basic values that dictate the choices we make (e.g., relationships, career). These choices reflect who we are and what we value.”

Yet, our sense of identity can be influenced by outside factors.

How is that even feasible? Well, Dr. Heshmat expanded, “Few people choose their identities. Instead, they simply internalize the values of their parents or the dominant cultures (e.g., pursuit of materialism, power, and appearance). Sadly, these values may not be aligned with one’s authentic self and create unfulfilling life.”

So, “Who am I?” I have always known that retorting to this question would require self-reflection, self-realization, the humility to accept my limits, my flaws, my fears, and mainly, the courage to look inward at my darkest realm where the demons are prowling, but until now I had not realized that I was not prepared to answer it. Currently, I am eager to go!

I took inspiration from Marcus Aurelius' Meditations 7.48, where he stated, "How beautifully Plato put it. Whenever you want to talk about people, it’s best to take a bird’s-eye view and see everything all at once." From now on until the end of this chapter, I have decided to refer to myself in the third person. While it may seem strange, addressing myself from an outside perspective allows for a more objective view, enabling me to detach from emotions and biases. By adopting this unique approach, I seek to explore my thoughts and feelings with a fresh perspective, unearthing insights that may have been previously concealed. Embracing the third-person perspective becomes an exciting, introspective journey that holds the promise of uncovering hidden depths and embracing a new sense of self-discovery. Ditching the "I" for "he" gives me a bird's-eye view of myself and my life.

On the morning of 8th September 2022 (this is the day he had the stroke), he was a 46-year young Italian. He was born and raised in Rome. He was a successful aeronautical engineer, working as senior manager in the engineering department of Etihad Airways in Abu Dhabi (United Arab Emirates) since January 2013.

He had had several job experiences before then. All in the technical, engineering side of aviation, and for the last 15 years in the Middle East and North Africa (MENA). If asked, “Was he a workaholic?” he would utter, “Yessssss!” He loved his job; mainly the feeling of accomplishment he got every evening when leaving the office, knowing he had given his best for the organization and the people he was working with. Returning to work after the stroke, he had to change this attitude—stress is harmful to stroke survivors and people in general. He had finally understood that he could not sustain that pace anymore for his well-being. Many studies have confirmed that chronic emotional distress (e.g., depression, anxiety, post-traumatic stress) is common in stroke survivors.

“Can stress cause a stroke?” In the aftermath of his stroke, he started searching for an answer to this relevant question. Later, he discovered that as highlighted in a 2016 study titled "The Emotional Stress and Risk of Ischemic Stroke," conducted by the Polish Neurological Society, it is evident that both short-term acute stress and extended chronic stress could elevate the likelihood of experiencing a stroke. The research underscores that stress impacts the cardiovascular well-being of the body, potentially causing alterations in blood pressure and the blood's ability to clot. These changes in physiological factors have the potential to heighten the risk of stroke.

At the time he suffered the stroke, he oversaw three sections in the engineering department with twenty direct reporters. He was promoted to manager in late 2014 and senior manager in early 2022. His role was to enable his team to perform at their best for the greater good of Etihad Airways. He was an enabler—the compound that kept his team together and helped them to excel and give their best. He always tried to give his best as well. He liked exploring novelties to improve their work. A few years earlier, he started learning coding (e.g., data science and machine learning) to improve his teamwork. He identified opportunities by automatizing some manual tasks via the development of simple python scripts. His aim was reducing his team's manual work, so they could focus on their core role as aeronautical engineers. Over the years, he worked to foster a family, rather than a team of highly skilled professionals. His motto was, ***"We win, and we lose together, no matter what!!!"***

He separated from his spouse seven years ago, and for the past six years, he has had a new life partner, Lei. Despite the separation, he maintained a friendly and amicable relationship with his ex-wife, Monica. Therefore, she wasted no time in coming to Abu Dhabi on the same day of his accident, along with his sister. Together, they managed most of the administrative, medical, and support tasks he required during the first two weeks. Monica has never failed to provide her support when he needed it. Either to help him with the relationship with his son or a word of support during his rehabilitation.

He was an amateur mountain runner with a dream to run and complete a 100km mountain race in 2023. Today, it is still his dream, but now, he is not even close to the optimal physical condition required to pursue that dream. Honestly, he is also not sure if he would have ever been ready. However, he will keep working hard to one day be able to conquer those mountains. Although, today with his current physical limitations, even a light jogging is difficult, almost impossible without the fear of tripping at every step, so you can imagine running!

Figure 2- Gathering of the Abu Dhabi Striders before a mountain race in the UAE.

He liked reading books. His preferred genres were history, politics, Greek mythology, ancient moral stories, and philosophy, especially Stoicism. He was also interested in religions and their teachings. Mainly the great monotheistic, including Hinduism.

He also loved cooking (his art name was *"The Naked Chef"*), particularly Japanese and Korean cuisines, and he could not miss out Italian. His specialties were all kind of fresh pasta, homemade pizza, Japanese ramen, assorted starters, grilled fish, and pork.

He found pleasure in travelling, mainly in Asia, and spending his free time together with his running club mates, especially running and camping in the mountains and deserts of the UAE. He was having a rather good life overall. He was financially solid, usually risk-averse when dealing with investments and personal finance. He would consider himself somehow happy; although, he always had some interior struggles to reach inner peace, fighting self-doubt and rebuilding a broken relationship with his son, Gabriele, who was 19 years old at the time.

Since his separation from his wife, he has faced a challenging relationship with his son. Their communication has been troubled, and he was struggling to maintain an open and honest connection. Along the years, difficulties arose, hindering their ability to understand each other and share their feelings.

If he had to imagine a glass containing water only to the halfway point, he would instinctively view that glass as half empty! He was a pessimist by nature, with more negative than positive thoughts about the present and the future. He characterized himself as a "cosmic pessimist," drawing inspiration from the book, *Cosmic Pessimism* by Eugene Thacker (2015). In this work, Thacker asserts that pessimism represents the most basic form of philosophy. While many associate pessimism with a personal disposition or mindset, it is also a philosophical concept. In this context, pessimism represents a worldview asserting that pain and hardships are inherent to life and existence.

At the forefront of philosophical pessimism stands Arthur Schopenhauer, a notable 19th-century German philosopher. Schopenhauer suggested that the human would lack inherent purpose and could never truly be satisfied.

Although pessimism is generally classified as a wholly negative personality trait, it can provide some benefits. There are the benefits of having a mindset known as ***"defensive pessimism."*** He had always used pessimism as a planning tool because he had the tendency to experience anxiety about the future. It gave him a sense of control by imagining and then taking measures to be prepared for potential negative outcomes or the worst possible scenario of a situation. He was aware that there is a fine line between this strategy and allowing anxiety to run wild and predict all manner of dangers or problems. In his case, defensive pessimism meant being realistic about the fact that things do not always go perfectly and preparing for some of those possibilities ahead of time.

But he saw that he was missing the best time of his life in his present. Besides the self-induced stress, he was also struggling with work-related stress. They affected his mood and sleep, every day. He was in a state of low dopamine production, resulting in fatigue, mood swings, low focus, insomnia, and intense caffeine cravings.

With his new companion, Lei, he had a good relationship. They shared many interests together, such as running, travelling, and reading. They had many dreams about their future together. They relished defining themselves as "Partners in Crime."

The following words capture what he thought about her. He wrote them to her a few years earlier:

"In this modern world where alienation, ressentiment, and individualism are the pandemic byproducts of today neo-colonialism,

A flower seed was planted in a remote area, unknown to most.

Amid wretched conditions and the general aloofness, this seed strenuously battled to break the hard crust of the individual's emotions.

Ultimately blooming in all her beauty and sheen,

Conveying sustenance to the needy and touching the hearts of many.

She thrives with the belief that doing some good for others is not a burden, but a pleasure,

That faith is a relief for troublesome souls and that our destiny is written in the stars.

Her inebriant scent gives peace, and her smiles give joy to the ones lucky enough to overlap their paths with hers.

Touching her petals provides unrivaled sensations.

She is a rare and wonderful flower who reminds us that humanity is not doomed, and happiness can still be found in this modern world."

Moreover, in 2022, he experienced a few physical problems, to which he did not give the right importance. There were no yearly checkups or routine blood samples to check his overall physical status. He assumed he was healthy. His accident, however, helped him to understand that he was quite careless with his health over the last few years and to not discard any alarm his body gave him.

Perhaps, to better understand who he was on the morning of his accident, you must first understand the existential path he followed to reach that point in his life, because for every today there is a yesterday.

During his youth, he had been a conundrum of unsolved existential queries, a desperate and solitary mix between Don Quixote and Cyrano. He struggled to provide answers to the world around him, with the hope that having ideals and ideas would possibly be something good. But the main struggle was to define that "something good," to make sense to the estranging society he was part of.

He would experience the feeling of not being enough. To demonstrate at any cost that he was valuable.

He would feel alone and lonely every minute—nothing would bring peace to his torments. He would find comfort only when immersed in reading or scribbling words on a paper. They would make him escape his reality like in psychedelic voyages. They were different parallel levels of his reality to which he did not want to belong.

He would immerge himself in reading Russian literature, such as Dostoevsky, Chekhov, Gogol, and Tolstoy; Martin Luther King, Malcom X and Nelson Mandela; the great revolutionaries of the past, Che Guevara, Simon Bolivar. He would read about history and politics. Initially, he admired anarchy and communism. With the years, he would change such interests, to be replaced by economics, philosophy, psychology, and coding.

He would also start writing; scribbling was a means of relief where he could loudly scream everything he wanted, be himself for once. He was someone with many ideas, someone who wanted to smile at life, enjoy, love someone, talk, debate, write poetry, solve the problems of the world, cry when required, leave people better off, understood, accepted for whom he was, not forced to fit into society.

But as much as he tried to fight, to remove the grey, the despair and fragility from his world, he felt defeated, never in control, never really at peace with himself and with his demons. Thus, he decided to die inside, align to the conventional society protocols, becoming one invisible drop in an ocean filled in by ignorance, shallowness, and triviality.

Now, if he looks back, all that happened because he had never trusted himself, never self-realized his potential, and for too long, he had bent to the rule that had to fit in that society, locked in the box. These have been oblivious years spent surviving rather than living.

He was someone who did not like the society he was living in and most of the people with whom he was sharing the same planet. He preferred to be alone rather than in the company of people who could not give him anything in intellectual terms. He was also someone full of emotions, ready to remove the rational brake when required.

He could be light and dark, night and day, gentle and supportive, but at the same time, cold, distant, pragmatic, and indifferent if required. Someone that did not believe in love as our consumerist society wanted to sell it. Someone that believed that intellectual relationships were the ultimate fruit of our evolution. Most probably a byproduct of it. And possibly the only real differentiation between us and animals and our ancestors. Someone always looking for answers. While he acknowledged the presence of a higher power and appreciated the teachings of various religions, he resisted extreme interpretations. He believed that some individuals used religion as a justification for their actions against others. He envisioned a harmonious world where people from diverse religious backgrounds and ideologies could coexist peacefully.

He was someone who did not accept any concept for granted; no dogma, always looking for the exception and confirmation and flaws in the theory. Someone longing for a simple life and internal peace, who does not care about glamour and appreciates trivial things. Someone in need of challenges. Someone that, by looking at a person's eyes, could read their soul.

Deep down, he never liked who he was. Pessimistic, almost catastrophic. Overthinker. He used to be self-critical and put a lot of pressure on himself: "I should be losing weight." He had lots of mental filters. He mainly focused on the negative aspects of life. He used to magnify the negative and minimize the positive. However, he was looking for inner peace. He wanted to accept his own limits and work hard to learn, to strive to become better.

It has been a long and difficult journey to reach that point. Now he can tell you with confidence and conviction who he really was on that morning. This is also the first time he has said such things, being fully honest and transparent, even with himself.

This is Where it All Begins

"Where is my right arm?" I voiced my concern to Lei who was around me with my friends. I had completely lost awareness of my right side. It was like my arm was not attached to my body anymore. I could not feel it. The lost awareness of my right arm made me comprehend that there was something wrong with me. At the beginning, I mistook it for heat exhaustion or mere fatigue. As time passed, I realized it was something more profound and complex.

"[...] In the middle of the journey of our life, I came to myself, in a dark wood, where the direct way was lost. It is a hard thing to speak of, how wild, harsh, and impenetrable that wood was, so that thinking of it recreates the fear. It is scarcely less bitter than death: but, to tell of the good that I found there, I must tell of the other things I saw there... I cannot rightly say how I entered it. I was so full of sleep, at that point where I abandoned the true way. But when I reached the foot of a hill, where the valley, that had pierced my heart with fear, came to an end, I looked up and saw its shoulders brightened with the rays of that sun that leads men rightly on every road. Then the fear, that had settled in the lake of my heart, through the night that I had spent so miserably, became a little calmer. And as a man, who, with panting breath, has escaped from the deep sea to the shore, turns back towards the perilous waters and stares, so my mind, still fugitive, turned back to see that pass again,

that no living person ever left [...]" There are no other suitable lines to picture my current situation than quoting The Divine Comedy by Master Dante Alighieri (1308-21).

To give a bit more perspective, prior to my stroke, I was an amateur mountain and ultrarunner (you already know this from the previous chapters). As most of you already know, Abu Dhabi, the place I currently live in, is located on an island in the Persian Gulf, off the Central West Coast. Abu Dhabi is the capital of the United Arab Emirates, after Dubai, and its majority is desertic and flat. Thus, it is not the perfect landscape to train for mountain running. However, there is an artificial sandy hill, Al Wathba Birdcage Hill 30 minutes from Abu Dhabi with 120 meters of elevations from base to top. We ran it up and down several times during each training session. That is to build elevation to replicate the conditions of a typical mountain race. This allowed us to train and prepare our bodies and minds for the challenges of the race's demanding terrain.

La ***"Divina Commedia"*** is usually held to be one of the world's great works of literature. Divided into three major sections—Inferno (Hell), Purgatorio (Purgatory), and Paradiso (Heaven). The narrative traces the journey of Dante from darkness and error to the revelation of the divine light, culminating in the Beatific Vision of God which perfectly resemble my ride with the stroke from cover-to-cover meaning.

Let us analyze the initial paragraphs:

"In the middle of the journey of our life, I came to myself, in

a dark wood." This represents my life and my actual runs in Birdcage (Al Wathba Birdcage Hill, Abu Dhabi) where I was doing most of my runs. Also considering that I would later have a stroke while running.

"I came to myself, in a dark wood, where the direct way was lost. It is a hard thing to speak of, how wild, harsh, and impenetrable that wood was, so that thinking of it recreates the fear." This is the phase where I had my stroke.

"But when I reached the foot of a hill, where the valley, that had pierced my heart with fear, came to an end, I looked up and saw its shoulders brightened with the rays of that sun that leads men rightly on every road. Then the fear, that had settled in the lake of my heart, through the night that I had spent so miserably, became a little calmer." This is my mental and physical rehabilitation journey with highs and lows. It was like I was spending my days riding an emotional roller coaster until I was finally able to stop the negativity bothering me! What do I have to do to shake you off? I would keep repeating it to myself in my head up until I finally perceived that "The devil is not as black as he is painted" (Dante Alighieri, *The Divine Comedy*), and life can be beautiful and happy even after a stroke if we put in the work to change our attitude and thinking about life and its situations. As much as they appear difficult and heavy, like the feeling of having a knife in our throat while slowly lining toward the blade, there is always a possible solution and way out from our problems if we believe it and we put in the work.

As an amateur ultrarunner, I have always thought of myself as a warrior, a fighter ready to get back on his feet after a stumble or a fall (in this case an authentic fall to the ground and the consequent stroke) to cross the finish line.

"When life knocks you down, get up and fight back!" This was the line of the narrator in my head after I was out of the ICU, finally awake and aware of my surroundings, in a conscious state ready to put order to my thoughts after surviving an ischemic stroke.

But let us not put the cart before the horse and let me walk with you through my story.

Everything started on the morning of September 08th, 2022. The day started out like any other in Abu Dhabi for me. As usual, I woke up at 4 am, just a few minutes before the alarm went off. It was Thursday and we got ready for the usual running session with my running team, Abu Dhabi Striders, in Al Falah area. It is a desertic area five minutes driving distance from Al Reef, the neighborhood where I was living in.

At the time, I had just started the tapering phase of my training, meticulously preparing for the Budapest Marathon, which was set to take place at the beginning of October, a mere few weeks away. The excitement and anticipation were palpable as I honed my physical and mental readiness to tackle the challenge ahead. And that was not all, as I had also set my sights on another goal—the Abu Dhabi Marathon in December.

The evening before, I was feeling tired, but I did not pay much attention to my body, trying to warn me that it was sore, with low energy, probably exhausted from lots of running in the previous weeks. Just a few days earlier, four to be precise, on September 4th, I ran 62km at an indoor endurance race (the aim was to run the longest distance over a 7-hour period), where I snatched the third overall place and second place in the male category. It was my first time to be on a podium. Perhaps, if only I had listened to my body that evening, I could have stayed in bed and rested that morning, and my life could have taken a different path that day.

I have been haunted by this regret for long time until I was able to consciously acknowledge that the past is in the past and to not let it affect my here and now. The only viable path is ahead of us. Moving forward is the only option to pursue and the best way to move forward is to not dwell on the past or what went wrong. We should invest in actions rather than outcomes by appreciating the process and any small progress along the way.

My run started as usual at 5 am, like many other times for the previous three years before that morning. I was with Lei, Kevin, Jovi, Saif, Adele, Sophia (Fia), and Charlie, the mascot of the group. After the usual group picture, we went off for an easy 10km in the desert. Little did I know at that moment how the day would unfold for me.

Figure 3- Marco (second on the right) ready to start the running session on September 8th, 2022.

As the new day began, Apollo, the powerful sun god, started his important work. The sky started to brighten with soft colors like pink, orange, and yellow. The sun slowly rose above the horizon, spreading its warm and golden light. Everything started to wake up and feel the energy of the morning. It was a beautiful beginning to a new day.

That area was a landscape of sand, characterized by its flatness, harsh sunlight, and cracked land. The tracks left by cars were visible, alongside patches of dead grasses. The wind howled and rattled as it passed through the sparse shrubs, mimicking the sound of trampled leaves being crunched and crackled underfoot. In the distance, the barking of dogs blended with the sounds of cars driving on nearby roads. If fortunate, one might have caught a glimpse of the elusive Arabian red fox.

In that arid setting, the air was heavy with dust, with the taste of sand grains filling our mouths like crunchy snacks. Consequently, our mouths felt dry and sticky, and our saliva became stringy or thick. The air carried the scent of our own sweat and body odor. Additionally, there was a piquant smell of tomato sauce coming from the adjacent palace workers' kitchen. With our mouths open, gasping for air, we could inadvertently swallow some flying insects. As we used to run side by side, our conversations interlaced with our strides. Local and foreign politics ignited debates, everyday life stories unfolded, and sports stories fueled friendly banter. With each step, we exchanged thoughts, ideas, and laughter. Our shared runs had always been a platform for connection, where diverse topics merged, strengthening our bond.

When I got back to the car at the end of the training session, I chucked my torch, and after taking a last sip of water, I ditched the water bottle on the hood of my small car. Loudly, I told Lei who had already completed her session, “Last 200 meters for me today.” These were the last words I can consciously remember speaking that day, and these would be the last two hundred meters I run for a long time, probably a very...very... long time!

I started running, and after 150 meters, I felt unwell, so I stopped to assess the situation. I felt dizzy and almost passed out. I felt lightheaded, like I was going to faint any second soon. I allowed my body to fall on the ground so I could rest and recover. It was like falling from a great height. Fia almost stumbled over me while querying, “Are you ok?” I answered, “Yes, just feeling tired.” Now, I just guessed that it was my brain being starved of blood and oxygen that made me feel dizzy.

I do not know how, but somehow, I found the force to stand again and tried to go back to the car. After a few dramatic steps, I fell again. This time, my legs buckled, and I crumpled to the ground. I could feel the energies gushing forth from my body like blood spurting from a wound. I knew there was something wrong with me, but I could not imagine that I was having a stroke. It could have been a heat-stroke, because it was early September and summer was still in full swing in Abu Dhabi and the weather that morning was still quite warm.

I was on the ground, and as soon as my friends noticed me lying on the road, they sprinted toward me. I could hear their voice while rushing toward me and asking me how I was doing.

I was disoriented, I was having issues with perceiving my extremities. They made me a comfortable nest on the floor, and they tried to give me some water. I tried to raise my right arm, but I noticed that it was not responding as it was supposed to. There was no movement. At all!!

My friends got worried, and they rushed to call emergency response. The ambulance was quite fast arriving, although they had some trouble finding that place, because it was far from the main roads. The quick arrival of the ambulance saved my life, most probably!

I will be forever thankful to my friends for being by my side on the toughest day of my life. Their ability to recognize the severity of my situation and respond promptly likely played a crucial role in that life-or-death scenario. It was a testament to the importance of having caring and perceptive friends who can provide the support and assistance we need during challenging times.

While we were waiting for the ambulance to arrive, I recalled that place was the one where back in summer 2020, during the COVID-19 Pandemic, Lei and I met Kevin for the first time, the Abu Dhabi Striders captain, and Jovi, his soon-to-be wife. However, it would take another year for us to officially join the Abu Dhabi Striders running club. The inaugural run was held in May 2021 at Al Wathba Birdcage Hill.

After their arrival, the paramedic noticed right away that I was experiencing facial droop, which is one of the initial signs of a stroke. My right eyelids and the corner of my mouth appeared pulled down, and I was unable to smile or speak clearly.

Therefore, they started asking me questions to assess if I was having a stroke. One of them asked me, "What's your name?" and I responded, "Marco," in my perfect English with a strong Italian accent (to understand what I am referring to, watch the video *The Italian man who went to Malta*, which can be found on the Internet. It is good for a laugh!). He continued, "Where are you from?" I said, "Italy." Then he asked me to repeat three different words after him, which I found so difficult. I was only able to pronounce a few syllables. Then he asked me in sequence, "Raise your right arm," "Raise your right leg." I was able to do it only once and after that no movement was evident on my right side.

After a few other questions and checks, the paramedics threw me an unexpected curveball by saying, "You are having a stroke." They were talking to me and my friend in such a way to convey the seriousness and urgency of the situation. It was a loud wake-up call for me.

I got sick the way Hemingway says you go broke: "gradually and then suddenly."

I could feel my skin tingling as sweat formed; my sweat-stained t-shirt clung to my body while I was mentally ordering myself to calm down and relax. I was doing rapid lip movement as I was trying to find the right thing to say or answer to my friends and the paramedics. I had a sensation of pounding in my ears and uncontrollable body tremors. I was having images of what could be flashing through my mind like hypnagogic hallucinations.

I am Fuck@d, I told myself and I vented all my frustration in Italian in my head. At that point, I was more annoyed than worried by the situation. As the Budapest Marathon loomed just a few weeks away, a wave of doubt washed over me, casting shadows on my confidence. Doubts began to creep into my mind, and I found myself questioning whether I would be able to stand at the starting line.

In that instant, I felt so disheartened and detached from reality that I even told Lei that after the ER visit, I would eventually have worked from home that day, because I could not imagine that I would be out of the office for the following five months.

Since the day of the accident, I have not returned to that place. However, I recognize that someday I will need to revisit it to find closure and make peace with the memories it holds.

SSMC

Hold on tight as we zoom into my adventure at Sheikh Shakhbout Medical City (SSMC)! Buckle up for a rollercoaster ride through this chapter of my life (from September 8th, 2022, to September 23rd, 2022). I recount the highs, lows, and everything in between during my hospital stay. Prepare for a thrilling tale, where the unpredictable reigns supreme, and hopefully, you will also have some good laugh.

ENTERING HOSPITAL

*What the f*ck is happening to me? Will I recover and how long will it take?* As soon as the paramedics loaded me into the ambulance—boom—those questions took off, bumping around like a pinball in my head. Door closed. Safety belt latched. And we were flying to SSMC. There, I would spend two weeks until being declared out of danger and discharged. When laying in the ambulance, I started assessing myself and questioning my state, but I had no definitive answer yet because I did not know anything about stroke.

We arrived at the emergency room and a parade of doctors, nurses with green/blue scrubs, and visitors welcomed me. I could hear doors sliding open and shut coming from every direction, the ventilation air exchanger, screams, cries, moans, gasps, grunts/hisses of pain, people talking in low voices, intercom calling out codes/directions, squeaky wheelchairs, as well as the clicking of each keyboard stroke under the light and heavy typing styles of nurses and doctors.

Right away, I noticed a different smell profile. It was bitter with an undertone of the fragrance contained in soaps and cleaners. The area was filled with the aroma of lightly burned coffee. The emergency room resembled an organized circus. It had lots of activity and a sense of controlled chaos.

The rooms had ventilation, but the air felt still. There was no fresh air allowed; like in many hospitals, the windows do not open. Every time I am in a hospital, I recollect touching the cold metal bed rails, the soft pillow on which my head was resting, and crisp sheets on which I had laid for months.

I was reading all the signs, especially the ones with small letters. I wanted to self-confirm my brain was still functioning. I was also verifying if I was taking too long to answer a question or respond to the doctors' questions. I was engaged, but I was avoiding eye contact as a sign of my increasing discomfort with my situation.

In the ER, doctors and nurses started again with a complete assessment, e.g., questions and movements. My Glasgow coma scale which is used to classify Traumatic Brain Injuries (TBI), was 15 (mild head injury).

In the ER, Lei battled with terror and anxiety, yet her reserved nature compelled her to mask her emotions. Despite the tempest within, she presented a facade of calm composure. She endured the situation in silence. Her actions spoke louder than the words she could not find.

After the initial assessment, they sent me to do a CT scan and CT angiogram. The scans confirmed ischemic stroke owing to left ICA dissection with occlusion by thrombus. My blood pressure and vitals were normal, and my blood glucose was within range.

As per standard medical protocol, I received intravenous thrombolysis. Cerebral angiogram confirmed that I had occlusion and dissection of my left ICA. There was evidence of blood clot and severe narrowing at the area of the dissection. The doctors performed an angioplasty on my groin to open and enlarge the artery.

Doctors decided not to put a stent because it required immediate therapy antiplatelet. I received thrombolysis to break up the blood clot, to avoid risk of internal bleeding; hence, antiplatelet therapy was not recommended. Unfortunately, the thrombolytic therapy did not help to recanalize my distal artery, and I was finally moved from the Angiogram Suite to the ICU to track my condition.

The evening settled on my first day in the ICU. I confronted death, emerged victorious, and stood as a living testament. I was ready to tell my tale of resilience and triumph. For some obscure reasons, I knew my destiny was to inspire others with the power of survival. Through that tragic event, I felt the universe was whispering wisdom to me. It gave me lessons amidst the turmoil. It urged me to be strong and find resilience. And I discovered the transformative power that lies within the depths of adversity.

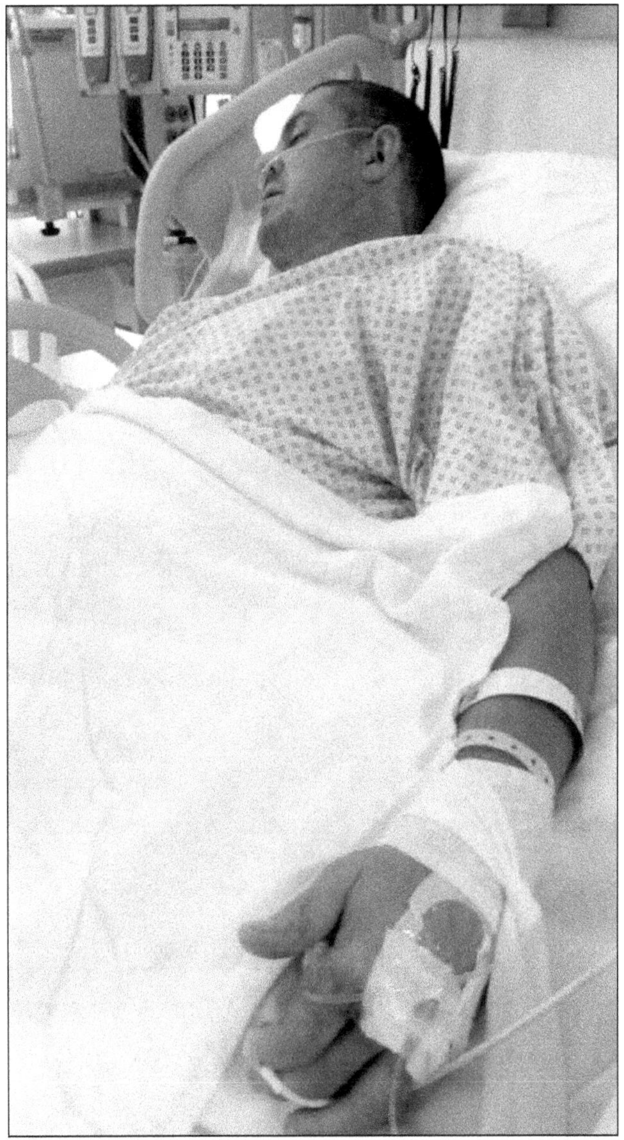

Figure 4 - Marco right after emerging from surgery.

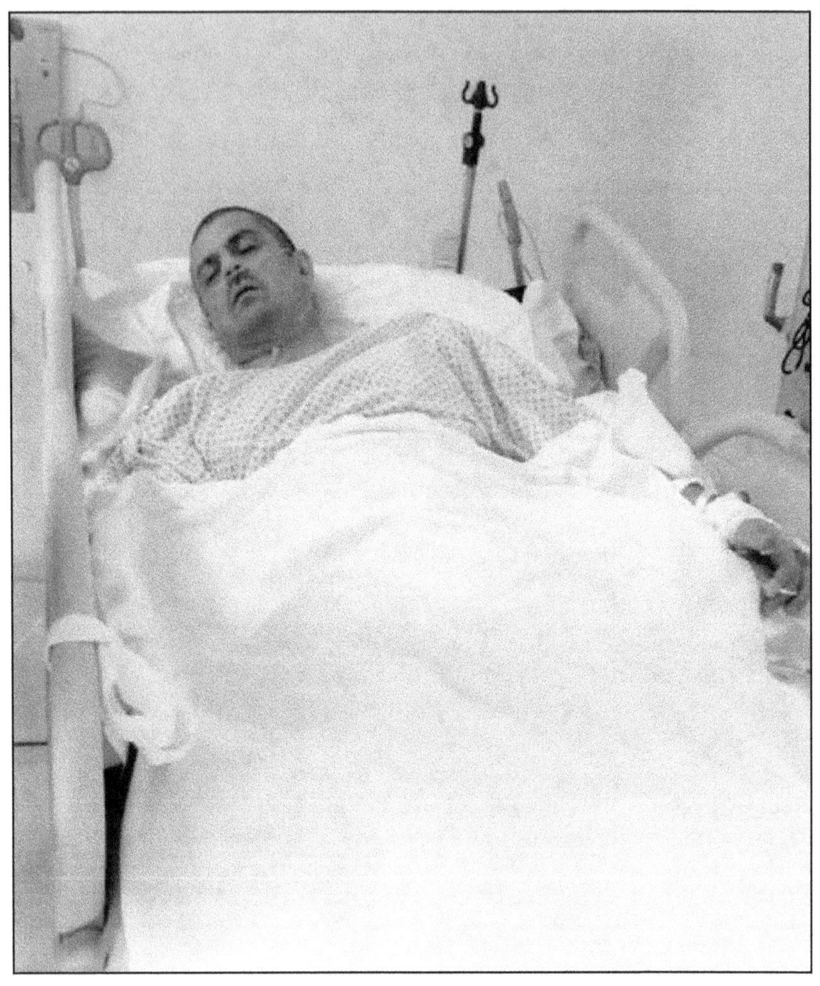

Figure 5- Marco right after emerging from surgery.

A Miracle in the Science Realm

"Is there any chance he will make it through the day? I am so scared for him!!" my sister questioned the doctor in charge, who answered back, "I completely understand your fear and anxiety. Medicine is a science, and we cannot always predict the outcome in every situation. We are using all the available treatments to support your brother's condition. But the severity of his condition makes it challenging to predict with certainty."

Upon my transfer to the ICU, the medical staff opted to conduct a fresh round of CT scan and MRI. The new results corroborated the previous findings. Dissection and blood clot in the superior part of my left ICA. Additionally, the findings showed that the left side of my brain had blood supply from the right side.

The ischemic stroke occurred due to left artery ICA dissection. It involved a tear to the artery wall. The tear led to the formation of a blood clot or thrombus. It completely blocked the artery, resulting in reduced blood flow to the brain. So, the cerebral cells in the left hemisphere of my brain perished. This triggered an inflammatory response. It led to the leakage of fluid and proteins into the brain tissues. Hemorrhagic transformation is the name of this condition. Additionally, the accumulation of this fluid caused brain swelling or edema. It could further worsen the damage and lead to increased pressure within the skull.

Elevating the bed's head and blood pressure monitoring were the means to take care for the hemorrhagic transformation and edema. Besides, I was also given mannitol. It is a diuretic and helps to produce more urine, so you can lose salt and excess water from your body. It also treats swelling around the brain. The left side of the brain was affected. It resulted in a weakness in my right upper and lower limbs with associated right facial weakness.

I also had mild dysarthria (difficulty of speaking). The muscles used for speech were weak. But luckily enough, I had no dysphasia (how to speak and understand language).

The day was as fuck@d as it gets!! I would have screamed aloud if only I still had the ability to speak at that moment.

I cannot imagine where my body found the energy to survive that first day in the ICU. This incident tested me in unprecedented ways, unmatched in my lifetime. Friends and coworkers of all religions and beliefs, offered heartfelt prayers. They were all praying for my survival. Their earnest hopes wove an invisible thread of support. I have no doubt that the power of those prayers pushed me through those traumatic initial days in the ICU, helping me to defy the odds and nurture the flickering flame of life. Over the course of these months, many people told me, "It was a miracle. God has given you a second chance on this planet to live a new life, and you should not waste it. Embrace it as much as you can."

By this time, my faith had long since slipped through my fingers, lost to the tides of time. But this very accident would serve as a transformative moment. It would reshape the very core of my beliefs.

The memories of my first day in the ICU remain hazy. Sedatives and medication enveloped me, encouraging rest and recovery. As I fought between life and death in the ER, dramas unfolded in the hospital corridors and in Italy. At 9:14 am, my friend, Masoud (my Omani brother), sent a message on the WhatsApp group (Etihad with Fun). Masoud, Ashraf (my Sudanese brother), and I have had this group for many years by then. The connection shared among us three can only be explained as that of brothers.

From the moment we met 10 years ago, there was a connection that went beyond being colleagues and friends. We formed a tight-knit trio, like *The Three Stooges*. We navigated both personal and professional challenges together.

Figure 6- Marco (center), Masoud (right), and Ashraf (left) standing beneath an aircraft at work.

We were there for each other during good and bad times. We rejoiced in each other's triumphs and offered comfort during difficult moments. Like brothers, we had each other's backs, offering solid loyalty and trust. We worked side by side, collaborating on projects and exchanging ideas. We were pushing each other to excel. We knew each other's quirks, strengths, and vulnerabilities. We accepted them without judgment. Our nickname encapsulated the dynamic and humor that defined our relationship.

Like the famous comedic trio, we brought laughter and mischief wherever we went.

We had our WhatsApp group for gossiping, updating each other about everyone’s availabilities, and to call for a coffee break during working hours. That morning, they were looking for me to have breakfast together like every day. I was known to always be an early bird in the office until that day, which changed my life.

Within the realm of our morning rituals, we formed an exclusive Breakfast Club. Ashraf curated tasty dishes that adorned our table, while I provided the elixir of life itself—authentic Italian espresso. This club emulated the exclusivity reminiscent of the triumvirate, the Trimurti. The Hindu gods Brahma, Vishnu, and Shiva, representing creation, preservation, and destruction. Specific colleagues were privileged to be invited on occasion, granting them entry to our sanctuary. Outsiders craved to join our club, yet they remained forever on the periphery.

Another cherished tradition shared between the three of us was the yearly Iftar at Ashraf's place. Iftar, a significant occasion during the holy month of Ramadan for Muslims, symbolizes the breaking of the fast at sunset. Each year, Ashraf's wife, Hind, dedicates herself to preparing the feast in a traditional Sudanese iftar style. The warm ambiance and the inviting aroma of delectable flavors create a delightful setting for our gathering.

Among the dishes, my all-time favorite is the mouthwatering chickpea falafel. The allure of these falafels has become so irresistible that they are now my most desired food even for our daily office breakfasts. Falafel is a Middle Eastern dish made from ground chickpeas or fava beans, combined with herbs and spices. As we come together to share this delightful spread, the bond of our friendship strengthens, and the essence of Ramadan envelops us in a profound sense of unity and joy. These treasured moments are etched in our hearts forever, reminding us of the power of shared traditions and the enduring camaraderie between friends.

With Hind's association with New York University in Abu Dhabi, her support goes beyond just being a friend. Later, she would be instrumental in helping me acquire the electro stimulator, a crucial addition to my hand rehabilitation strategy that Metha and I agreed upon.

From my phone, Lei texted back that I was at the hospital after falling ill during the morning run. She also broke the news, letting them know, "He is on procedure right now. An artery torn while running, causing blockage." It was a big shock for Masoud and Ashraf. They were in denial and disbelief, asking themselves, "How has it happened to Marco?" In the eyes of everyone, I was healthy and fit. I was the one running almost every morning before work. That is a question some of my colleagues still bring up from time to time. They justify their unhealthy live style. "If it happened to Marco who was healthy and fit, it can happen to everyone, at any moment."

The news of my accident spread across the office by word of mouth and texting. Everyone was dumbstruck by the news and wanted to come to the hospital to check on me as soon as possible. This, because, like Ashraf summarized it, "Marco is very lovable by all; he is very popular." At work, I always followed the mantra, "Lead by example." I always tried to share, help everyone, and to be the best version of myself. I believed, "Cooperation beats confrontation." These are the reasons why I received so much love and support from friends and colleagues. As such, colleagues and friends started flocking to the hospital to check on me.

My popularity in Abu Dhabi is something that has left an impression on my sister and parents. They will bring it up from time to time, especially about when I received visitors at the hospital and at the rehabilitation center. The same morning, when I was in the ER, Lei suggested that I inform my sister, Marzia, and my parents back in Italy. I tried to avoid it because I was still hoping my accident was not so serious and it could be resolved. Anyhow, Lei did not agree with me. When the medical team brought me to the Angiogram Suite, she tried to contact my sister. Unfortunately, they were facing issues on understanding each other in English. Luckily, my friend, Christian, had arrived at the hospital from the office. Thus, he explained the situation in Italian to my sister. My sister was so surprised that she was at a loss for words. She felt a tingling in her chest and a clenching stomach while trying to digest Christian's report. On the phone, she had struggle speaking, producing only choppy sentences. Still in shock, Marzia went to inform my parents. She started speaking, not letting my parents get a word in. My parents were overwhelmed by the disturbing news. They were unable to focus and control their emotions. Their voices were choked by tears. My father was the most confused. He tried to open his mouth, but nothing came out. My mother tried to remain more composed, but her mind started racing in search of answers. They were in denial by questioning the source and the facts.

Christian kept a communication line with my family. For the entire day, he provided updates to my parents as the medical teams released them. They also contacted Monica to let her know about my accident. Monica and my sister agreed to fly to Abu Dhabi on the same day as the first available flight. My sister had her passport expiring within six months; hence, she could not fly the same day. She asked a personal favor of a friend to have an emergency renewal of her passport. They renewed her passport on Thursday. So, Monica arrived in Abu Dhabi on the evening of the day of my accident and my sister arrived the following day. Monica and my sister managed the continuous flow of visitors like two traffic cops. They talked with doctors and ensured I was looked after at the hospital. In the two weeks I was at the hospital, they also went the extra mile, helping me with the exercises for my mental and physical rehabilitation.

I have blur recalls of the ICU room. It was quite dark for most of the day. The room had dimmed lighting. The darkness reduces sensory stimulation and allows patients to rest and recover. But there were various machines and equipment present in the room, essential for monitoring and supporting the patient's condition. I have some vague recollection of the alarms and beeps coming from those machines. They were roaring in my ears, disturbing my rest. Everyone had in mind a question that evening: "Will Marco be able to survive the first night with the hemorrhagic transformation and edema in the left side of his brain?"

The hemorrhagic transformation and edema could have significant consequences after my ischemic stroke. Hemorrhagic transformation increases the risk of neurological deterioration. It could worsen the severity of the stroke and would require specific management strategies. The accumulation of fluid known as edema could exacerbate brain tissue damage. It could elevate intracranial pressure. Moreover, it may lead to the emergence of further issues, such as deadly brain herniation.

Yet, at that stage, no doctor was in the position to provide a resolutive answer. I was like the character of the painting

“Landscape with Charon Crossing the Styx” by the Flemish artist Patinir. Dated 1515-1524, it depicts a classic subject from the Aeneid (Virgil) and Inferno (Dante). Charon (the central figure) ferries a human who is deciding between heaven and hell. In my case, I had to decide between life and death, and I decided on the former.

So, Friday evening brought my sister who was keen to visit and offer her help. As my sister entered the ICU room, she approached my bedside with a mix of anticipation and concern.

As she came closer, I was holding a piece of paper in my left hand. When my sister placed her hand close to me, a surge of emotion overcame me, causing me to drop the piece of paper. With a firm grip, I held onto my sister's hand, seeking help, reassurance, and comfort. My sister believed that despite my appearance of sleep, the act of holding her hand had a deeper truth. My brain was alive, and my spirit was present. To my sister, I was always present. Even though I could not communicate, she knew I was there. I was talking through subtle nods. Each day, as visitors shared their thoughts and questions, I would respond with either a nod or a shake of my head. I was acknowledging their words with silent understanding. Even if I was silent, my eyes spoke, conveying gratitude, empathy, and connection.

Due to the edema, my inability to close my eyes created the illusion of perpetual wakefulness. My condition hindered normal eyelid function, causing them to remain open, despite exhaustion.

During my week in the ICU, an influx of visitors brought immense comfort and support. Friends, coworkers, and colleagues streamed in. Even Rami, my direct boss, and Paul, the SVP of Etihad Technical. They provided all possible support from Etihad and their personal ones to me and my family. Despite the number of visitors, my sister and Monica, recognizing the potential strain, orchestrated the visits with meticulous care. They worked tirelessly, managing expectations, and providing updates to everyone. Their diligence shielded me from excessive fatigue. They ensured that each encounter was meaningful and uplifting.

Among the countless visitors who would come to see me, there were two people I never refused to meet, Ashraf and Masoud, my dear brotherly friends. Regardless of the circumstances or my state of mind, I always welcomed their visits. Our bond was unbreakable, forged through years of shared experiences and solid support. Their presence always brought comfort and relief during my most challenging moments. Their friendship was, and still is today, a beacon of light. It reminds me that no matter how dark life may seem, there will be someone who stands by your side.

On the morning of the third day, I was still in the ICU, when the doctors gathered my sister and Monica to discuss my condition. The medical professionals projected the MRI scan of my artery onto a screen. They highlighted the dissection and the occlusion by thrombus. The images painted a stark reality of the danger lurking within.

With non-technical words, the doctor explained how difficult my situation was. They revealed that intervening to remove the blood clot carried immense risks. It was behind my left ear, close to vital areas of the brain. Such an operation, they cautioned, could lead to dire consequences. It could have left me with only slim chances of survival. Faced with this dilemma, the doctors outlined their decision: To administer medications that would aid in the clot's solidification and then disappearance. They recognized that it was a delicate equilibrium depending on the synchronicity between the body's natural healing processes and medical treatment. Moreover, the doctors expressed their hopes that the edema would reabsorb. This was crucial to reduce the pressure on my brain and remove me from imminent danger.

Throughout their explanation, the doctors remained empathetic and compassionate. They were doing everything to manage my condition. They asked me to remain optimistic while understanding the gravity of the situation.

During the initial days in the ICU, I was unable to consume solid food due to my weakened state. As I regained awareness and presence by the third day, I started drinking protein shakes, following the doctors' prescribed regimen.

I have limited recollection of the first days in the hospital's ICU. They are like fragments of a shattered reflection. This phenomenon is known as retrograde amnesia. It can impair the retrieval of memories formed before traumatic events. Some individuals may recollect certain memories over time, while others may experience partial or incomplete memory recovery. Memory retrieval depends on various factors such as the extent of the trauma, individual resilience, and the effectiveness of therapy.

I was awake to eat and speak with doctors, family, and friends from time to time as I explained earlier. Doctors' words were like a sharp object puncturing a water balloon. Their words were gushing out in a wave of emotion when they were speaking to me. As they explained what happened and the possible consequences, I thought about the worst-case scenarios: *Will I remain paralyzed? Will I be able to use the right side of my body again?* These mind-blowing questions would pop up in my head when I was awake. They left me with a feeling of uncertainty about my future. This led me to have anticipatory fear and to overthink the possible outcomes of my situation. I was trying to look positive to the outside world, but inside, I was in turmoil. I was devastated. Nowadays, I have accepted that life is full of uncertainty and worries about the future. Many things are outside of my control. But my mindset is key to cope with difficult circumstances and facing the unknown.

Every night, between 2 and 3 am, they will bring me to the radiology department for a sequence of MRI and CT scans. These examinations focused on monitoring the status of swelling on the left side of my brain. The hospital corridors whispered with hushed footsteps because of the timing. They would wheel me into the sterile room, surrounded by diagnostic equipment. I recall navigating the corridors. I would read all the signs, especially the ones with small letters to assess my cognitive abilities. In the elevator, anticipation would fill the air as we made our way to the scanning room. With the aid of a sliding sheet, the medical team transferred me from the bed to the scanning machine.

The nurses knew the significance of this event. They would always perform this task with care and precision. They wanted to ensure optimal imaging of the affected area. A symphony of clicks and hums would resonate through the room. The machine capturing detailed images of my brain's intricate pathways. Inside the machine, I would ponder the potential results and glance around. I was hoping to recognize some familiar faces among the medical team. When the scanning was over, the nurses would bring me back to the ICU room to rest and sleep.

After a difficult week in the ICU, the doctors determined that I had reached a stable yet critical state. The timing was perfect for the beginning of the next stage of my healing process. With cautious optimism, the doctors moved me to the Stroke Unit. There, I would start the intricate journey of rehabilitation. The Stroke Unit provided the care to address the challenges posed by my conditions. To signify my ongoing critical condition, a yellow band was placed around my wrist. Its vibrant color served as a visible reminder for the medical team. It symbolized the need for heightened attention and care. The yellow band functioned as a beacon, signaling to all who saw it that my journey to recovery was far from over.

As I pen this chapter, I am overflowing with gratitude towards my extraordinary sister, Marzia, Monica, and Lei, for their tireless care during my days in the ICU. Their dedication to my well-being extended far beyond expectations. They tended to my needs. They ensured that I received proper nutrition by feeding me with love and patience. Their gentle hands and meticulous attention ensured my personal hygiene. They brushed my teeth after every meal. Moreover, they provided me with therapeutic massages and exercises to my legs to reduce discomfort and promote circulation.

Stroke Unit

"It was better for Marco to remain paralyzed than for his brain to stop functioning. If that were the case, it would be better if he did not survive this stroke," my sister kept repeating over and over during my rehabilitation. Since the first day, her main concern was for me to regain full brain function.

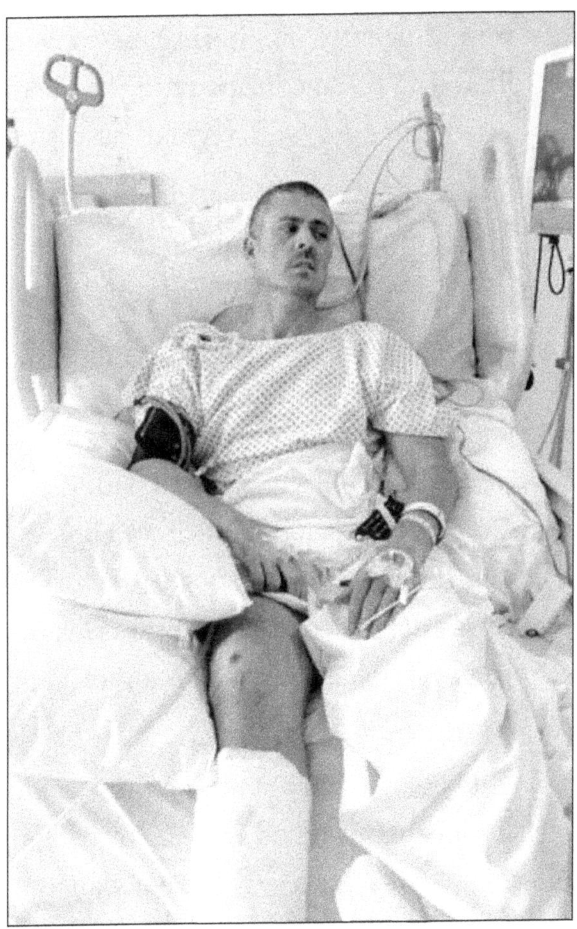

Figure 7- Marco at the Stroke Unit, where his journey towards recovery began.

As I transitioned to the Stroke Unit, the doctors gave instructions that I needed to remain motionless, particularly with my head, to facilitate the ongoing reduction of my brain swelling. The nurses collaborated closely with my loved ones, implementing a range of interventions. They kept adjusting pillows and positioning me to provide optimal support to my motionless body and minimize the risk of any potential strain. They were diligently monitoring my movements and ensuring I adhered to the medical advice. Medications were administered meticulously, and regular assessments were conducted.

During the initial two days spent at the Stroke Unit, I went through an incessant rollercoaster of mood swings. I experienced moments of profound sadness and depression, followed by sudden bursts of happiness accompanied by relentless laughter. Doctors attempted to provide an explanation for these peculiar behavioral patterns by likening my brain to a computer undergoing a reboot. Just as a computer needs to undergo a reboot to restore its normal functioning, it was described that my brain was undertaking a similar procedure of resetting and recalibrating itself after the stroke.

My sister would later tell me about one rather embarrassing comic sketch because of my mood swings. Once, I found myself experiencing heat waves like a lady in menopause. As a result, I would attempt to remove my hospital gown, unknowingly exposing my adult diaper. To my rescue, my sister would diligently monitor the situation, covering me up whenever doctors and nurses, particularly the female ones, came to deal with me. It was a comical yet slightly mortifying scene. Despite the humor in retrospect, it highlights the vulnerability and the need for support during such moments.

My appearance after the stroke was like that of a boxer, displaying noticeable physical effects like facial drooping and a black eye. Furthermore, my upper limb was completely immobile and there was limited movement in my lower one. As I tried to shift positions, a persistent throbbing sensation would spread across my entire body. It served as an indicator of my delicate condition caused by the stroke and of the considerable time, I had already spent confined to that hospital bed.

From the third day, which was the 10th since the stroke, I gradually started regaining awareness. Waking up proved to be a challenge. It was like the worst hangover I had ever experienced. My memory was hazy, and I could not remember much of what had happened.

When I was finally awoken, I was faced with the unforgiving, clinical glow of the hospital room and its snow-colored barriers. As my eyes were fully open, I directed my attention to my surroundings. I felt a sense of comfort and familiarity from the fresh, pristine sheets under me, while the mattress was firm but surprisingly cozy. I was surrounded by the familiar scent of antiseptic commonly found in hospitals, and the gentle hum of medical machinery.

From my room, I was able to perceive far-off conversations and the subdued movements of medical staff. The ambiance was bustling yet serene, a delicate harmony between rush and understanding. A wave of uncertainty, anxiety, and a slight sense of fear immersed me as I attempted to put together the events that had taken place.

However, I discovered comfort in the company of the people who were important to me. Their presence helped me feel less isolated. The path ahead would be challenging. But with my strength and resilience, and the support from my loved ones, I was ready to work toward my recovery.

The room was arranged to accommodate a single patient. The area was generous and well-equipped to ensure a pleasant experience, with the added convenience of a sleeper couch for a potential overnight assistant. Through the large window, my eyes could glimpse the neighboring residence situated in Shakhbout City, triggering a flurry of imaginative thoughts in my mind, each idea sparking another.

I have a recollection of a bothersome incident. The loud and persistent alerts emanating from the various monitoring devices affixed to my body. A variety of data was collected, including readings from heart monitors, blood pressure monitors, and ECG monitoring devices. The sudden onset of warning signals emanating from the machine I was connected to caused me immense fear. Either the blood pressure or heart monitor would sound an alert time to time, starting with a soft tone and escalating to a loud, piercing tone, which would also activate an alarm in the nursing control room. Therefore, the nurse would rush to my room, often conveying the same message, “The machine seems to be malfunctioning as the alarms are triggered on our monitoring screens, but it appears that you are in stable condition. Our team aims to resolve the issue and potentially replace the equipment to prevent further inconveniences to you.” In the end, maintenance tried to repair the monitoring devices, but they ended up replacing them to ensure that no more false alarms would arise again.

The alarms were also a disturbance to the nurses. Recent research indicates that a substantial majority of alarms—ranging from 90% to 99%—that activate on inpatient wards are erroneous, leading to a phenomenon known as "alarm fatigue" among medical professionals. This phenomenon causes healthcare workers to become desensitized to the sound of alarms, posing a significant threat to seriously ill patients who may need immediate attention from overworked and jaded staff. Fake alerts can also induce anxiety among patients and their loved ones, who are abruptly thrown into a state of heightened alertness, unsure if the sound they are hearing indicates a real crisis. As commonly understood, stress can have detrimental effects on our well-being, particularly when already in the vulnerable state of being hospitalized.

In the morning after breakfast, it was my habit to peer through the window and observe the ongoing events outside. Typical of the area, the steady stream of vehicles would be moving sluggishly along the narrow streets. Loud noise would be produced by a multitude of automobiles varying in their form, dimensions, and colors. In contrast with the rest of Abu Dhabi, the area that I was hospitalized in lacked tall buildings or skyscrapers, except for the hospital itself. That area was primarily occupied by short-rise homes that consist of individual detached houses. These residences are commonly built with one to three stories and offer around 180 to 450 square meters (2,000 to 5,000 square feet) of enclosed floor space, which is usually sufficient for their occupants' needs. Moreover, there are villas and townhouses available to cater to the housing needs of big families, alongside a few other buildings, with a range of two to five stories, exclusively designated for apartments of different sizes, accommodating a significant section of the expatriate working population.

Many houses in warm countries were originally constructed to allow for natural temperature regulation. The architectural features of small openings, mashrabiya pierced screens, enclosed outdoor spaces, and wind-catching towers characterize the design. The traditional means of construction were adept at controlling sunlight exposure and facilitating air flow. The old-fashioned Arabic houses possessed a delicate charm and a warm ambience. Those contemporary residences draw on the architectural and artistic heritage of the UAE's traditional Arabic homes as a source of inspiration for their construction and aesthetic elements.

Most of these residences are built from materials obtained from the surrounding area. The houses tend to integrate seamlessly with the environment, exhibiting natural shades such as dusty tan, brick-red, or soft gold. A popular design characteristic often observed is the existence of level roof structures. The utilization of a flat roof design has multiple functions, such as gathering rainwater during rare rainfall and creating an area for social events or an extra living space. While standing far away, you may perceive elaborate geometric shapes, intricate arabesque motifs, or decorative carvings embellishing the outer surfaces. These adornments depict the area's profound creative legacy and meticulousness.

The UAE, along with other countries in the Arab region, are primarily known for their arid, scorching regions. Contrary to European houses which welcome ample sunlight and warmth by keeping their interiors open, the Arab house boasts a more introverted design. In the Arabic household, the focus of daily life is directed towards an internal courtyard, rather than an external front garden that overlooks the street. From a distance, one might perceive these patios as unobstructed areas within the encompassing edifice. Private outdoor spaces are used by families for various purposes such as social gatherings, ventilation, and shade.

I could identify certain homes with elongated, upright shapes that resemble towers. These towers, called "wind towers" or "badgirs," were originally developed as a means of ventilation prior to the advent of contemporary air conditioning, but nowadays are only cosmetic artifacts. Traditionally, these towers were created to take advantage of prevailing winds, funneling them into buildings for natural cooling and air flow.

Moreover, it can be observed from a distance that the properties are enclosed by tall barriers such as walls or fences. There are measures in place to keep the interior areas concealed from public view. Similarly, limited-sized windows and openings enable ventilation and preserve confidentiality.

As I gazed upon the various houses, my mind was inclined to wander, and I found myself pondering the experiences and lifestyles of the inhabitants. I would begin visualizing the different people. Possibly, an individual was enjoying a peaceful morning without work. Someone could be engaged in reading a book, viewing a film or television series, or merely relaxing on the sofa. An individual might be creating a delectable dish. They could be testing out a novel formula or getting ready to whip up their loved ones' preferred meals. In an alternative residence, someone could possibly be engaged in diligent work or academic pursuits. They may be engaged in different activities such as typing on a computer, studying textbooks, or joining virtual meetings. The inhabitants of a different house may be actively pursuing their hobbies and areas of interest. They might be dedicating their time to activities such as exercising, playing musical instruments, or creating art. In certain households, people might be busy handling domestic tasks and running errands. They could be engaged in activities such as tidying up, arranging things, tending to plants, or performing maintenance duties. In my opinion, these options only scratched the surface, and there was likely a vast array of alternative and distinct possibilities. In the end, it was solely my mind attempting to envision the intricacies of the existences progressing in those residences visible from my vantage point.

Additionally, depending on the weekday, my thoughts would turn towards what my day would have been like prior to the accident, causing me some uneasiness and sadness. Inside, I would cry and scream. It is natural to contemplate previous encounters and ponder about how things would have turned out if certain circumstances had not taken place. I acknowledged that it was normal to experience such thoughts and feelings and granted myself the necessary time and room to work through them. Following the experience of those emotions, my intention was to adopt a cheerful outlook, banish any sorrow from within, and overcome the situation. The brief moments of happiness and anticipation would swiftly be replaced by sadness whenever I caught sight of my immobilized right arm and the inability to manipulate my right-hand fingers. After my morning meditation, I often found myself pondering my revised identity as I had suddenly transitioned from being an engineer, parent, brother, friend, son, and physically energetic individual to a stroke survivor.

After breakfast, a designated nurse would arrive to gather blood specimens. Typically, samples were collected from a surface vein located on the inside of my left forearm. The preferred target for collection is usually the median cubital vein within the arm. This is due to the proximity of the vein to the skin, as well as the absence of significant nerve clusters in the surrounding area, resulting in less pain and discomfort for the patient during the medical operation. Alternatively, the samples were obtained from the rear of my hand where there was also the IV that administered drugs into my bloodstream.

During the process, I trusted that the nurse would remain composed and comforting, prioritizing both my physical and mental well-being by following strict infection control measures and securing clean and safe surroundings for both of us. It was evident that the nurse was fully focused on locating the accurate spot for blood extraction, as that was a customary task for them.

After accurately aligning the needle, the nurse would secure the collection tube to the needle holder. Due to the absence of air pressure within the tube, blood was sucked into it. If numerous tubes were necessary, the nurse would replace them as required, taking meticulous care to guarantee that each tube was adequately filled and tagged. After gathering the required blood samples, the nurse would take off the tourniquet, extract the needle, and quickly use either a cotton ball or gauze pad to put pressure on the punctured area. Finally, in accordance with hospital regulations, the nurse would properly discard the utilized needle and receptacles in a designated sharps container.

As I observed the needle penetrating my epidermis, I sensed it restlessly navigating through the various skin layers in pursuit of the perfect vein to harvest my invaluable blood, akin to the search for a missing treasure. As I underwent a needle injection, I tried to connect with the needle and ponder over the orderly penetration of its tip through the various layers of my skin. In doing so, I aimed to alleviate any discomfort and conceal my grimace expression.

It was typical for me to respond to pain and discomfort by smiling. It has been demonstrated that smiling can evoke positive feelings and regulate negative ones. Research indicates that it is a commonplace response to display a grin or chuckle as a reaction to both psychological and physical discomfort. These studies suggest that individuals can use a smile to protect themselves from revealing their genuine feelings of emotional or physical distress. According to them, an alternative viewpoint regarding the act of smiling during moments of distress—either physical or emotional—is to perceive it as a form of masking. Individuals who are undergoing distress may not exhibit any indication of their predicament to others. Nevertheless, they are experiencing hardship. There can be an array of negative emotions hidden beneath a mask, such as sorrow, anxiety, apprehension, terror, and numerous physical discomforts.

During my days at the hospital, amidst the therapy sessions that played a vital role in my recovery, I found solace and diversion in the simple pleasure of doing some brain games like chess and checkers, trying to read, and watching TV. One day stands out in my memory; when I stumbled upon a Korean TV series centered around the fascinating world of pearl commerce in the picturesque Jeju island. As I lost myself in the intricate plotlines and mesmerizing shooting, a flood of memories washed over me, reminiscent of my first trip to Korea with my dear Lei, back in 2018. Nostalgia and reminiscence were overwhelming as I recalled the vibrant sights and the tantalizing aromas that enveloped us during our sojourn.

Ever since my transfer to the Stroke Unit, I had been considerably more alert and attentive to my surroundings. By engaging in meditation and introspection, I tried to examine and process the events that occurred and their resulting effects. I was fortunate enough to receive professional psychological assistance from the hospital that led me to acknowledge that the events that occurred were not my responsibility and were simply destined to happen. I reconciled with myself, while also committing to doing everything within my means to bounce back and regain my previous self or the perception I had of myself prior to the incident. While initially, I believed that I had fully passed through the final phase of sorrow, which is acknowledging and accepting the situation while retaining hope for the future, despite my determination to stay true to that mindset, a few months later, I found that it was difficult to put into practice, and I would begin feeling anguished, distressed, and with a tendency towards desperation. Through discovering new significance and direction in my life following the stroke, I will finally overcome these obstacles. However, this is a topic that I plan to discuss at a more appropriate time.

The experience of loss, be it the passing away or the suffering of a cherished person, or the experience of illness like a stroke, can inflict significant emotional harm and immobilize individuals. It can linger for an extended period. Discovering significance in defeat enables us to unlock a way towards progress. According to Kessler (2019), "Having a sense of meaning assists us in understanding and coping with feelings of sorrow."

Three days before my departure from the hospital, my parents arrived from Italy. They replaced Marzia and Monica, becoming my pillars of strength. Their presence extended for six months until I gained the confidence to live independently once again.

Similarly, my son, who was studying at a university in Rotterdam, Holland, made the decision to fly to Abu Dhabi for one week to be by my side and provide his assistance. It was a heartfelt gesture that touched me deeply, knowing that he was willing to take time away from his studies to support me during my recovery. Upon his arrival, my son transitioned from an art student into the role of a caregiver and supporter. He not only provided emotional support but also took care of my physical needs. One of the tasks he willingly undertook was feeding me. In addition to assisting with my meals, my son also played an integral role in my speech exercises. My son would guide me through the exercises and encourage me to articulate words and sounds. His presence made the exercises more enjoyable, and I felt motivated to put in my best effort.

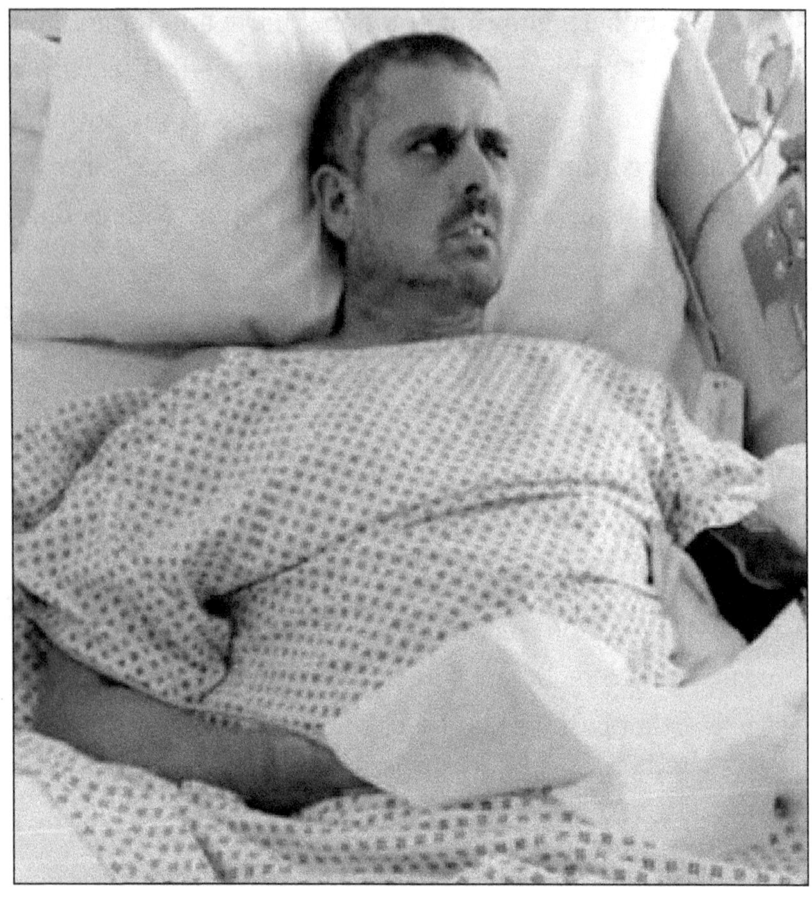

Figure 8- Marco's first fully awake day at the Stroke Unit.

TASTING NEW GROUND

"Repeat after me: A, E, I, O, U." Despite my deliberate efforts to repeat the letters as instructed by the therapist, I could not emit any audible sounds from my mouth. Regardless of my tries to vocalize the letters "A, E, I, O, U," no sound seemed to emerge. It was like trying to blow up a balloon, yet with the first breath, nothing occurred.

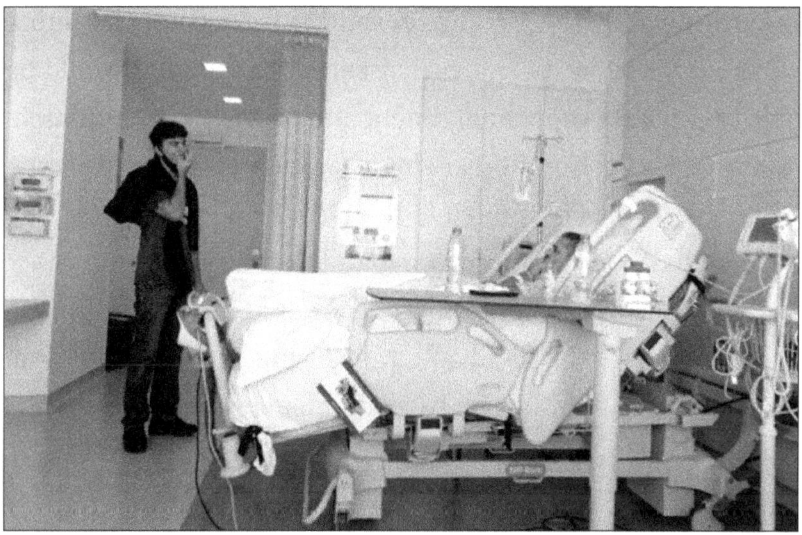

Figure 9- Marco engaging in speech exercises with his son, Gabriele.

On the third day at the Stroke Unit, the medical team decided it was the appropriate time to commence my rehabilitation journey. The first step involved assessments conducted by both the occupational therapist and speech therapist to evaluate my physical, cognitive, speech, and swallowing functions.

The occupational therapist began by conducting an initial check-up of my physical status. During the assessment, it became evident that there was general weakness in my right limbs, particularly in my right arm and hand. This weakness was a direct result of the stroke. To address the issue of my right hand being clenched, a condition known as hand spasticity, the occupational therapist recommended the use of a hand splint. The hand splint served a crucial purpose in keeping my fingers open and preventing them from remaining closed in a fist-like position. By wearing the splint, I would be able to promote proper alignment and prevent further muscle tightness and contractures. The recommendation to wear the hand splint was not limited to the Stroke Unit but would also be adopted later during my rehabilitation at the dedicated center. The occupational therapist would guide me on the proper usage of the hand splint, ensuring it was comfortable and properly fitted to meet my individual needs.

Additionally, the occupational therapist outlined a plan to help me regain the ability to walk. The first step was to assist me in sitting on the bedside and attempting to transfer to a wheelchair. By doing so, I would be able to accompany my family to the hospital restaurant and venture out of the room for the first time. The next step in the plan was to assist me in standing with the help of assistants and holding onto a walker for support. Once I was able to stand, the goal was to gradually start walking with the walker in the corridor outside my room.

At one point, to aid in the improvement of my cognitive functions, the occupational therapist arrived with a collection of engaging kids' games. These games were carefully selected to challenge various cognitive abilities, such as memory, problem-solving, attention, and creativity.

One of the games the occupational therapist introduced was the Buttons Boardgame. Its objective was to use colored buttons to recreate various figures. As I examined the patterns on the board, I analyzed the arrangement of buttons needed to replicate the figures. However, no matter how hard I tried, I struggled to create recognizable shapes. Even a simple straight line with just four buttons seemed beyond my reach. While frustration started to build within me, my sister grew increasingly concerned about my brain function. Despite her eagerness to assist me, the therapist intervened, instructing her to allow me to persevere on my own. It was important for me to keep trying and exerting effort to overcome the challenges.

A few days later, I found myself once again facing the Buttons Boardgame. As I began placing the buttons on the board, it quickly became evident that my progress was still limited. Frustration started to well up within me, and my mom wanted to help me. However, my sister intervened, recalling the therapist's words from our previous session. She firmly stopped my mom from intervening, reminding her of the importance of allowing me to tackle the challenges on my own.

Similarly, the speech therapist conducted assessments to evaluate my speech and swallowing functions. During the assessments, I encountered some difficulties, particularly during the first attempt to vocalize the vowels. It was scary to experience that initial setback, but the speech therapist remained patient and understanding. I became aware of the tightness in the muscles on the right side of my face and mouth. The tightness made it challenging to form words and properly articulate sounds. The speech therapist recognized this issue and incorporated specific exercises to target the muscles in my face and mouth. She continued to guide me patiently and provided me with various techniques to improve my articulation and vocalization. She provided gentle guidance on proper tongue placement and breath control, helping me develop the necessary coordination for accurate sound production. Through a series of exercises, I gradually started to regain control over my speech muscles and improve my ability to produce clear and distinct sounds.

In addition to addressing speech difficulties, the speech therapist also evaluated my swallowing function. Swallowing impairments, known as dysphagia, are common after a stroke. The therapist conducted various tests and observations to identify any difficulties or risk factors associated with swallowing.

Based on the assessment findings, the speech therapist devised a tailored treatment plan to target my specific needs. This plan included a combination of exercises to improve my speech, face, tongue, and throat muscle strength—swallowing techniques. She also recommended stretching exercises for my mouth and face. All of them to be done several times per day whenever I had time.

The following day arrived, and it was finally time for me to experience the freedom of venturing out of my room to the hospital coffee shop with my family. As I settled into the wheelchair, the cold metal frame against my body sent a tingling sensation through me. They wheeled me out of the room, making sure I had a warm blanket to cover me, particularly my right arm and leg. I was still struggling with circulation issues and my extremities remained cold. As we crossed the threshold and ventured beyond the confines of my hospital room, a surge of emotions enveloped me. It was as if I had transformed into a captive animal, longing to break free. Every fiber of my being was filled with a sense of anticipation. The world outside, though still within the walls of the hospital, held the promise of liberation and renewed possibilities.

As we ventured into the corridor, passing by the nurse control station, I felt a sense of curiosity and independence. Two female nurses were engaged in conversation and warmly greeted us as we passed. I responded politely, but my mind quickly returned to my own thoughts. We continued, reaching the elevators, and I peered out through the window, gazing at the highway that lay beyond the hospital walls. I watched as cars sped by, some moving swiftly while others traveled at a slower pace. The continuous stream of trucks resembled a long serpent, snaking its way down the road. Memories flooded back to me of my own days behind the wheel and I wished for the day when I would regain the ability to drive once again.

The elevator stood before me like a majestic drawbridge, a gateway to a new realm waiting to be explored. With a sense of anticipation, I watched as its doors opened. As I rolled into the elevator, the warm sun rays filtered through the windows. With each floor we descended, my excitement grew. When the elevator doors swung open, revealing the ground floor, a rush of exhilaration washed over me. In that moment, I felt a surge of childlike excitement, like a kid venturing to the playground for the very first time.

Entering the coffee shop, I immediately noticed its well-organized layout. The space was thoughtfully designed, featuring small tables for those seeking a quick bite and cozy couches for those desiring a more leisurely stay. It was a welcoming departure from the sterile hospital rooms, offering a warm and inviting atmosphere for patients and their families to enjoy quality time together. The aroma of freshly brewed coffee and the scent of baked goods and savory treats filled the air. It was a haven where conversations flowed freely, laughter resonated, and stories were shared. Doctors, nurses, hospital administrators, families, and friends sat around the tables, engaged in animated discussions and laughter. Patients, like me, savored the opportunity to escape the clinical environment and embrace a sense of normalcy. My family settled into one of the comfortable couches; I was in my wheelchair. I felt a profound sense of gratitude. The coffee shop provided a space where I could momentarily forget about medical procedures and therapies, and I could focus instead on the simple pleasures of togetherness and connection. As time flew by in the coffee shop, the realization that we had to return to the room began to settle in. Reluctantly, we gathered our belongings and prepared to make our way back.

Finally, the long-awaited moment had arrived—the time to stand and attempt to walk. In the hours before the therapist's arrival, I found myself immersed in a connection with my unconscious mind, visualizing my first steps and the feeling of regaining the ability to take a few steps on my own again. The occupational therapists approached me with a reassuring smile. With their assistance, I slowly rose from the bedside. I felt a surge of excitement and determination as I found myself standing on my own legs for the first time since the stroke.

I clutched onto the walker tightly, my hands gripping the sturdy frame for support. It provided a sense of stability and security, allowing me to focus on the task at hand. The therapist stood by my side, their steady presence instilling confidence in me. I took a deep breath, ready to take my first steps towards regaining my mobility. With hesitant but determined movements, I tentatively placed one foot in front of the other. The walker served as my anchor, providing the stability I needed to maintain my balance. The therapist offered gentle encouragement, reminding me to focus on the process rather than the distance covered.

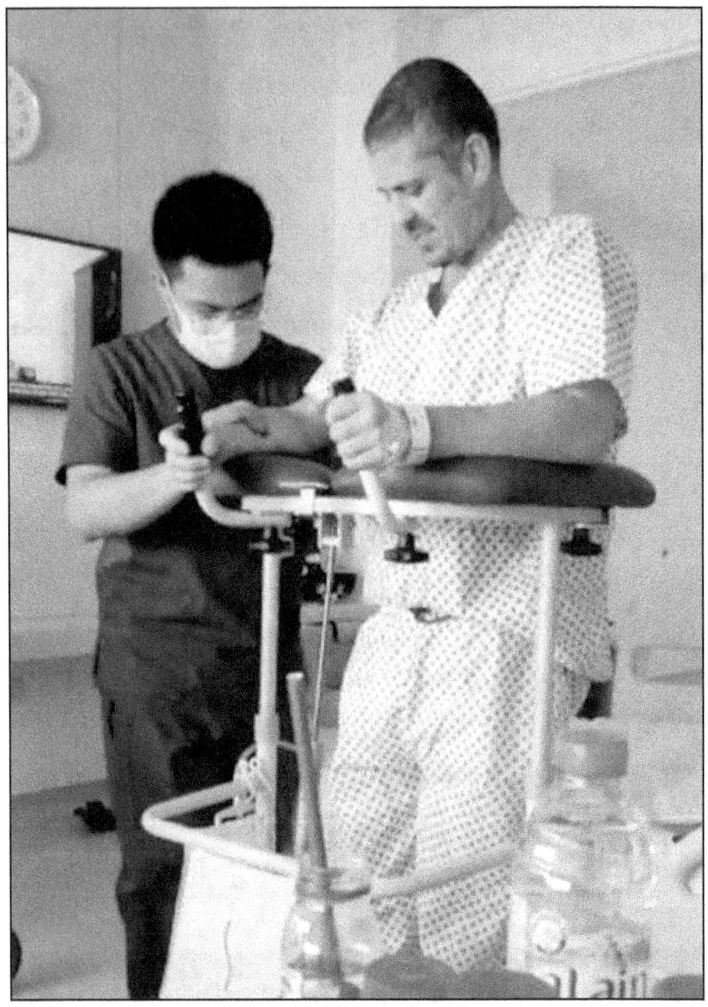

Figure 10- Marco standing up for the first time after the stroke, his hands gripping the walker for support.

As I attempted to walk, I noticed the significant impact the stroke had on my right leg. It felt stiff, almost like a rigid tree branch, making it challenging to bend at the knee. I could not sense the natural flexion of the joint, which made the act of walking feel foreign and unnatural. The therapist would carefully place my right foot in the correct position at each step. As such, I gradually started to distribute my weight evenly, allowing me to propel myself forward.

At that point, my conscious mind took over from my unconscious mind. I concentrated on gathering all my energies to regain control over my muscles and initiate movement.

Simultaneously, my left leg presented its own set of challenges. It felt weak, lacking the strength and stability I once took for granted. I relied heavily on the walker for support, using it as a crutch to compensate for the diminished function in my legs. Every step required focus and concentration, as I consciously tried to coordinate the movements of both my legs.

In addition to the challenges posed by my stiff leg, the stroke had bestowed upon me the condition of claw toes. They no longer responded to my commands, seemingly locked in a perpetually clenched position. They further hindered my movement and caused discomfort with every step I took. The lack of flexibility and control made it difficult to distribute my weight evenly.

Upon completing a lap in the corridor, a sense of happiness and accomplishment enveloped me. Exceeding my own expectations, I basked in the triumph of progress. The therapists guided me back to my bed, allowing me to rest and reflect on the steps I had taken.

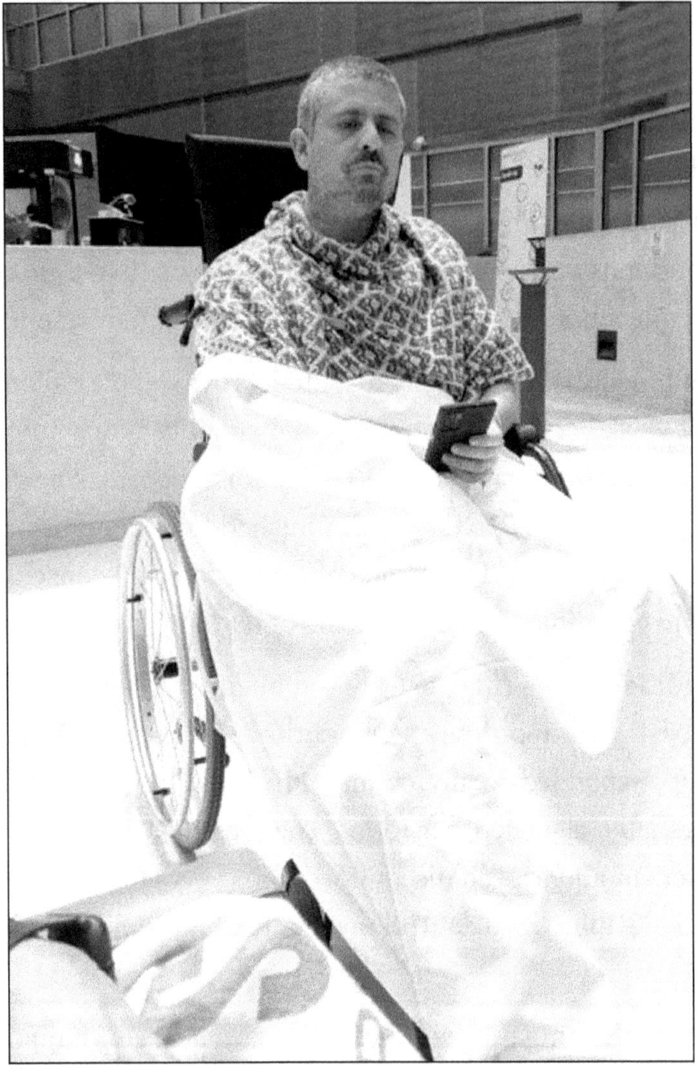

Figure 11- Marco venturing outside the room in a wheelchair for the first time.

THE BRAIN, THE MASTER PUPPETEER!!!

The human brain is complex. It is like a puppeteer guiding the movements of our body. Strings are the network of muscles and nerves that enable us to perform movements. Yet, when a stroke occurs, the control strings suffer damage. the coordination between the brain and the body is interrupted.

The brain is the command center, coordinating and regulating every movement we make. It communicates with the muscles and nerves, through electrical signals and chemical messengers. Imagine the brain as a conductor guiding the movements of a marionette. The strings are the muscles and nerves. They extend from the puppeteer's hand to the puppet's limbs. Each string carries specific instructions from the brain, relaying the desired action. When these strings are functioning, the puppet dances. They execute the puppeteer's will with precision and grace.

Yet, when a stroke occurs, it is as if the puppeteer's hands shake, causing damage to the control strings. The puppet's limbs, once coordinated and fluid, become unresponsive or erratic. This disruption arises from the stroke's impact on the brain's blood supply. It leads to a lack of oxygen and nutrients in vital regions responsible for motor control. As the control strings suffer damage, the connection between the brain and the extremities weakens. The puppeteer struggles to manipulate the puppet, and the once-fluent movements become hindered. Paralysis, weakness, or loss of coordination may manifest in different parts of the body.

The aftermath of a stroke is a complex journey of recovery. As a puppeteer must repair damaged strings, stroke survivors do rehabilitation to restore functions. Physical and occupational therapies play a crucial role, like the skilled hands of a puppeteer mending and reweaving the broken strings.

During rehabilitation, stroke survivors undergo exercises to rewire the brain and reestablish the connection with the control strings. Through repetitive movements, neuromuscular reeducation, and the activation of alternative neural pathways, the brain adapts and compensates for the damaged areas, restoring control over the extremities.

The process is akin to the puppeteer improvising, finding alternative ways to manipulate the puppet despite the damaged strings. Over time, the brain's plasticity allows it to create new connections and reorganize its functioning. This ability is called neuroplasticity. This is the same ability used to learn a new skill or subject.

Neuroplasticity, the brain's amazing adaptability, means it can change and grow. It is like a dance party in your head! Your brain rewires itself in response to experiences. It is like a garden where connections bloom and thrive.

To boost neuroplasticity, you can:

- Embrace novelty! Engage in diverse activities: painting, cooking, or learning a musical instrument. It is like a flavor explosion for your brain. Challenge yourself with puzzles and brain teasers. It is like a mental gym workout.

- Get moving! Exercise stimulates neuroplasticity. Walk, run, dance—anything that gets your body grooving. It is like a happy dance for your neurons.
- Feed your brain a healthy diet. Nourish it with omega-3 fatty acids, fruits, and veggies. It is like a feast for cognitive growth. Stay away from alcohol and caffeine as much as you can.
- Meditate and practice mindfulness. Focus on the present moment, here and now. It is like a peaceful oasis in your mind.
- Sleep well! Zzz... It is when your brain rejuvenates and strengthens connections. It is like a slumber party for your neurons.
- Socialize and connect with others. It is like a brain fiesta. Laugh, hug, and share stories. It is like a neural celebration.
- Reduce stress! Chronic stress is a neuroplasticity dampener. Relax, breathe, and find inner calm. It is like a soothing balm for your brain.

So, explore, move, nourish, meditate, sleep, connect, and de-stress. Your brain will thank you. Embrace the power of neuroplasticity and let your mind dance to the rhythm of growth and change!

LEAVING HOSPITAL

After spending a week in the hospital, the administration, in collaboration with my medical insurance, initiated the search for a suitable rehabilitation center to facilitate the next phase of my recovery. A few days after, on the morning of September 22nd, I was informed that the selection had been completed, and the insurance agreed to transfer me to NMC ProVita International Medical Centre in Abu Dhabi for in-patient rehabilitation on the following day. ProVita is the largest provider of post-acute care and rehabilitation in the UAE. They have services such as Long-Term Care, Post-acute Rehabilitation, Outpatient Rehabilitation, Home Hemodialysis, and Home Health Services for patients of all ages.

As news of my move spread, inquiries arose regarding my decision to persist my recovery in Abu Dhabi instead of going to Italy. In explaining my decision, I emphasized the advantages of staying in Abu Dhabi, including access to world-class medical facilities and specialized rehabilitation services. Another significant factor was the presence of Lei, along with my friends and workmates, who had been a source of vital emotional support until that time. I had taken that decision after careful consideration of my good health with the aim of achieving the best possible outcome for my recovery journey.

On the afternoon of that same day, two nurses from ProVita arrived at the hospital to discuss and organize my impending transfer to the facility. They demonstrated a profound understanding of the urgency and importance of my situation. From verifying medical records, including taking note of my daily medications to coordinating transportation, their expertise and diligence were evident in every step of the process. Before leaving, they informed me that they would be personally overseeing my transfer the very next day. Their presence displayed empathy and their actions spoke of expertise.

"Doctor, why did the stroke happen to me? I had no medical issues before, and even after the stroke, my health seemed fine."

"I understand your concern, but sometimes strokes occur without clear reasons, even when looking at your medical history. It is frustrating, I know."

"So, you mean it was just meant to happen, and there's no clear explanation?"

"In a way, yes. Sometimes medical science cannot fully explain why certain things happen. But what is important now is focusing on your recovery."

"Is there possibility I will fully rccover?"

"You suffered a severe stroke, and hence, it is less likely that you may fully recover. Anyhow, a complete recovery from a stroke is within the realm of possibility. Amongst those affected by a stroke, a notable 10 percent can achieve full recuperation, while a further 25 percent will regain their health with only minor limitations. A segment of patients (40 percent) may necessitate specialized attention due to more significant impairments, while 10 percent could require the resources of a nursing home or long-term care facility."

"Will I regain control of my right hand?"

"There's hope. With time and therapy, the brain can create new pathways through neuroplasticity, allowing you to regain control. However, it is hard to predict how long it will take. It could be a few months, years, or it may not fully recover."

On the morning of my departure, I had a good chat with the doctors about my neurological condition, its consequences, and the path to recovery. They also detailed the medications I needed to take daily. These included an antidepressant to support my emotional well-being, a medication to control cholesterol levels, another to treat constipation, and aspirin as a blood thinner. Aspirin would be a lifelong necessity to reduce the risk of blood clot recurrence. They ensured I had understood the importance of each medication for my ongoing health well. Additionally, they clarified all concerns I had about the post-stroke rehabilitation.

As soon as the doctor exited my room, tears welled up in my eyes. Their words laid bare the reality that the possibility of never regaining the use of my right hand loomed large. It was as if a lightning bolt had struck on an otherwise clear day. In that moment, it felt like the stroke had robbed me of my very identity. Little did I realize that only a year later, I would find myself thankful for the stroke for shaping my newfound identity.

In a moment of introspection, I made peace with myself and came to accept that running the Budapest Marathon was not in the cards for me at that time. Despite the disappointment, I embraced the reality of my recovery journey. While the thought of not participating in the Abu Dhabi Marathon also crossed my mind, I recognized that putting my well-being first was paramount. Instead of dwelling on what I could not do, I chose to focus on the progress I had made and the countless opportunities that lay ahead.

Later in the morning, as planned, the two nurses from ProVita arrived at the hospital to transport me to the rehabilitation center. With their assistance, I transitioned from my hospital bed to the ambulance stretcher. After completing the necessary paperwork, we proceeded to the service lift. We descended to the ground floor and as soon as we stepped out of the lift, a sense of déjà vu washed over me as I laid eyes on the ambulance parked just outside the entrance of the ER, the same place I used to enter that same hospital I was about to leave after two long weeks, which felt like an eternity to me.

The bright lights illuminated the ambulance's interiors, while the hum of the engine created a steady background noise. Inside the ambulance, each jolt reverberated through my body, amplifying my physical state. Every bump served as a stark reminder of my condition, evoking discomfort, and vulnerability. During the brief journey to ProVita, a mix of emotions washed over me. A sense of joy enveloped my being as I embraced the opportunity to continue my rehabilitation. Yet, a river of fear poured through my veins. Doubts clouded my mind about what lay ahead.

My parents had arrived early that morning at ProVita. They discussed with the administration to ensure a smooth transition to the new rehabilitation facility. Their presence provided a comforting reassurance, a familiar anchor amid change. We exchanged smiles and embraces, knowing that together, we would navigate this next chapter of my recovery. With their support and determination, I felt a renewed sense of hope as we embarked on this journey towards healing.

With the nurses' expertise, I was gently transferred from the stretcher into my assigned room, Villa 2 Room 6, which served as my initial residence at ProVita. Although designated for long-term pediatric care, it was temporarily allocated to accommodate my needs as the adult villas were fully occupied. I stayed in Villa 2 for just over a month until a room became available in Villa 3. There, I stayed for two weeks before finally being transferred to Villa 7, where I would stay until my official discharge on December 24th, 2022. The day that marked the end of my three-month journey towards recovery at ProVita.

At the age of forty-six, I lived a healthy lifestyle, free from smoking, with just a few drinks per week. I had no specific medical conditions, and there was no history of strokes in my family. For four years, I had been an avid runner, covering thousands of kilometers. However, life took an unexpected turn when, in an instant, a stroke nearly snuffed out my existence. It felt as though I had been transported into the body of an old man, grappling with a new reality—unbalanced, shaky, spastic, and burdened by half-paralysis.

Upon leaving the hospital, two important questions were still open: Did the blood clot persist, and was the artery still affected by dissection? The queries hinged upon the state of the blood clot, whether it had dissolved or persisted as a potential threat. Equally pressing was the inquiry into the artery's condition, whether the dissection had healed. As departure approached, the enigmas remained unresolved, casting a shadow of apprehension on the fact of avoiding a second stroke in the future.

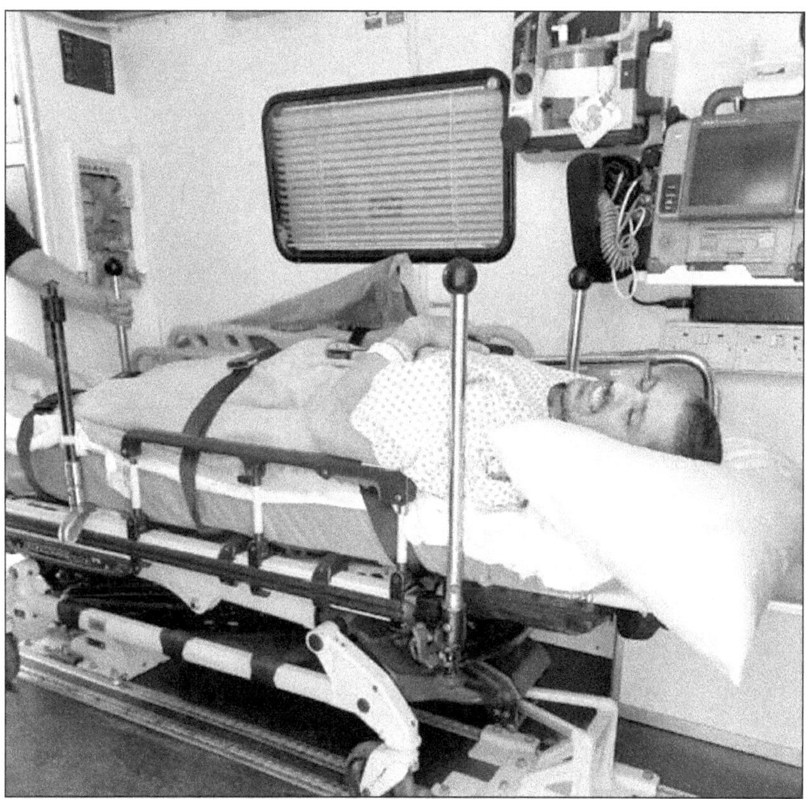

Figure 12- Marco being transported from the hospital to ProVita in the ambulance.

PROVITA

In this section, we dive into the significant period of my tenure at ProVita. It spanned from September 23rd, 2022, to December 24th, 2022. I wanted to present events in chronological order. But I had to rearrange the timeline in certain subchapters to maintain a coherent flow. You will learn the challenges and accomplishments encountered during my time at ProVita. Despite the altered timeline, I provide an overview of this pivotal phase of my recovery. So, let us explore the moments that shaped my experience at ProVita.

NMC PROVITA

I will always be grateful to the complete ProVita family for the support I received during my time there. They celebrated every milestone I had, no matter how small. They rejoiced in my victories and offered me support during setbacks. I reflected upon these words as I bid farewell to the ProVita team on the day of my discharge, ready to return home.

At ProVita, I experience the teamwork and dedication of the entire staff first-hand. The committed doctors, compassionate nurses, skilled therapists, and proficient administrators all played an integral role in ensuring the highest level of care and support.

ProVita had an exceptional group of doctors. The medical director, Dr. Ahmad Al Khayer, who is my doctor to this day, and Dr. Hussam Antwan Touma always took the time to listen and explain treatment options.

The therapists were instrumental in my rehabilitation process. They helped me regain my strength, mobility, and independence. They knew my challenges and goals, tailoring therapy programs to meet my needs. They guided me through exercises and provided me with unlimited support. The entire therapist team at ProVita was exceptional. Yet, I want to give a recognition to Metha and JD, who supported me throughout my three-month stay at the facility.

The nurses at ProVita were the true pillars of compassion and care. Their dedication to their patients was evident in their every action, from administering medications and monitoring vital signs to providing emotional support. They were not healthcare providers. They were beacons of comfort for patients and their families. Among the nurses at ProVita, I met exceptional individuals like Armie, Andre, and Karim. They had a remarkable ability to go beyond their professional duties. They treated me not as a patient, but as a friend. Their kindness, and compassionate approach made me feel valued. They cared for me in a way that went beyond the typical nurse-patient relationship.

Behind the scenes, the administrators at ProVita ensured a smooth operation. They took care of me. Reem and Mays created a welcoming environment for patients and the healthcare team. They allowed the team to focus on delivering the highest standard of care.

They also understood the importance of maintaining social connections during the recovery process. Reem and Mays ensured that I had the opportunity to enjoy outings with my friends. They managed the procedures, offering guidance and support every step of the way.

What set the ProVita team apart was their commitment to teamwork and collaboration. Each member recognized the value of their respective roles, and they knew the importance of working together. They communicated, sharing vital information and insights to ensure continuity of care. The interdisciplinary collaboration fostered an environment of mutual respect and trust. The team went above and beyond their duties. They demonstrated genuine care and dedication.

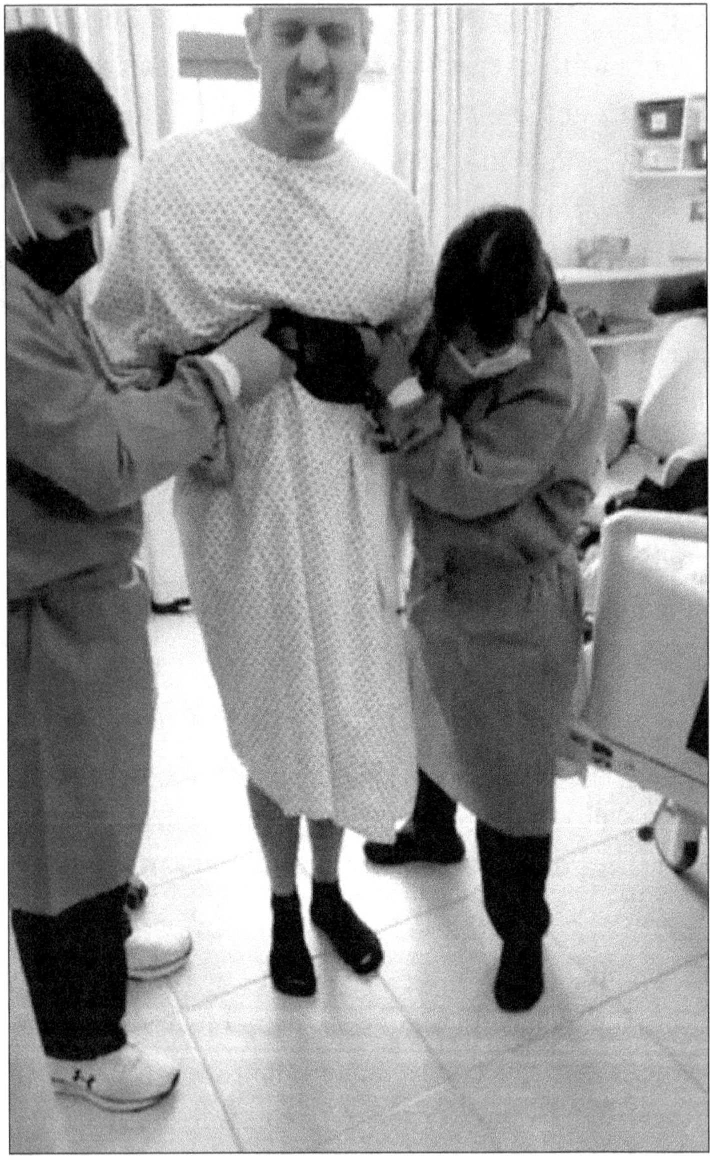

Figure 13- Marco attempting his first steps with the support of resolute nurses in his room at ProVita.

REHAB HAS STARTED

Embarking on the path to recovery marks the beginning of a journey that hinges upon the patient's dedication, persistent efforts, and diligent work. It is a voyage that demands commitment and a proactive approach to regaining one's health and well-being.

As I arrived at ProVita, I felt like the hospital had passed to the rehabilitation center the baton of my care. They performed the same initial assessment. The rehabilitation therapists delved into the nuances of my condition. The result was a comprehensive understanding of my needs. Their main goal was to assess my physical and cognitive capacities. They focused on assessing the movements and coordination of my arm, hand, and leg. They employed various techniques, utilizing standardized assessments and their personal clinical expertise.

The therapists initiated the assessment by encouraging me to move my arms and hands. My right arm and hand had minimal movement. It was indicating significant limitations in motor function. They documented the extent of my mobility restrictions. In contrast to the arm and hand, there was a greater degree of movement observed in my right leg. Yet, it became evident that I lacked control over my foot. The therapists noted the absence of precise movements and looked for any potential compensatory patterns that may have developed. The therapists also conducted evaluations of my sensory functions in my foot and arm. They assessed various sensory modalities, including light touch, vibration, temperature perception, and proprioception. The findings revealed diminished or absent sensory responses in certain areas. This suggested a disruption in the neural pathways from my foot and hand to my brain.

Due to my inability to control the movements of my right foot, I experienced a condition known as drop foot. To address this issue, the doctor prescribed the use of a foot brace called an ankle-foot orthosis (AFO). The purpose of the AFO was to assist in aligning my foot and provide the necessary support. The goal was to improve my gait and stability when I started walking. The AFO became an essential part of my daily routine, until I removed it after going back home.

To manage the risk of shoulder subluxation, therapists recommended wearing an arm sling consistently. Shoulder subluxation is common after a stroke. It involves partial dislocation of the shoulder joint due to muscle weakness. It causes pain, limited motion, and joint misalignment. Treatments include physical therapy, arm slings, and positioning techniques to enhance stability and restore function.

The sling provided much-needed support and stability to my weak shoulder. When I was lying in bed or using a wheelchair, I used a pillow as support. It provided additional comfort and prevented unnecessary strain.

On that same day, the speech therapist paid me a visit. She enquired about my hospital exercises. She advised me to continue with the exercises targeting the muscles on the right side of my face. During her visit, the speech therapist also inquired about my swallowing abilities. She assessed my swallowing function. She provided guidance on exercises and techniques to improve and manage any difficulties. At last, she determined that my progress in regaining proper speech was good.

The findings served to design a treatment plan tailored to my conditions. They told me that post-stroke rehabilitation can range from three months to one year. They emphasized that the catalyst for recovery is the patient's commitment and determination. Despite the initial challenges observed, the therapists remained optimistic on my recovery. They stressed the importance of consistent therapy and the potential for improvement.

As the sun descended on my first day at ProVita, I made a promise to myself: "Within a month, I will leave this place and return to my old life." But, when the end of the first month arrived, I was not ready to go home, so I revised my promise, extending it to three months. In the end, I managed to fulfill that revised promise and achieve my goal.

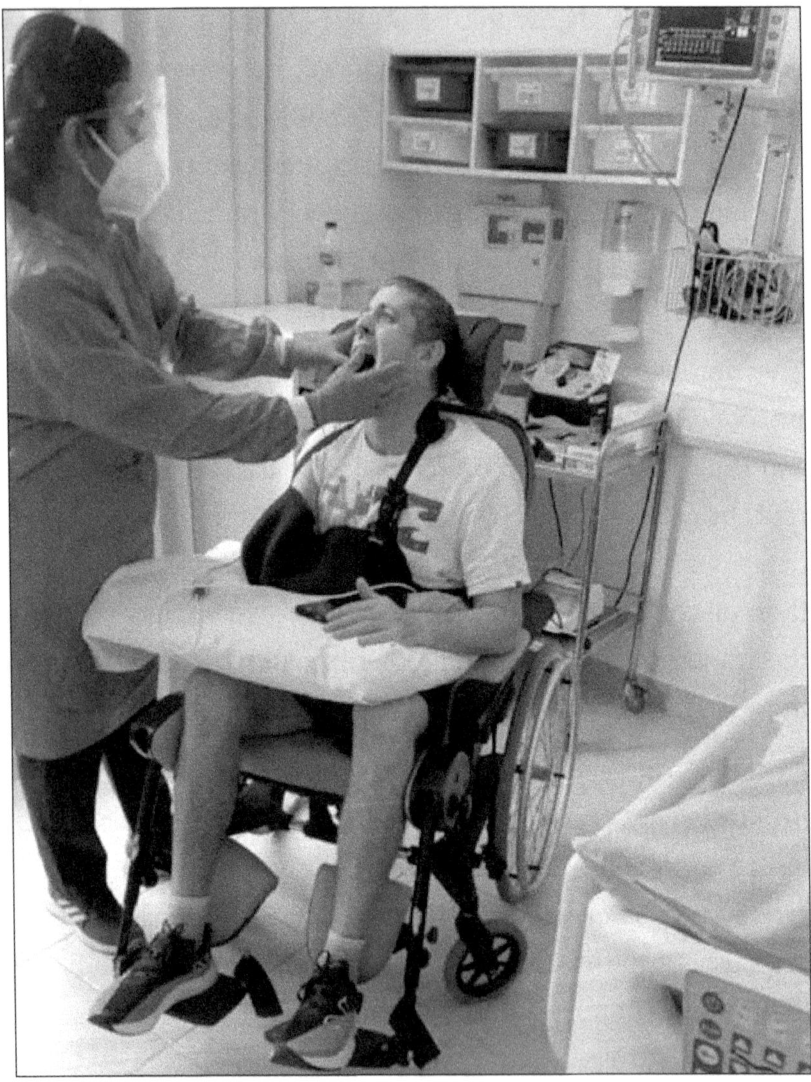

Figure 14- Marco engaged in his speech therapy assessment

Days in ProVita: Embracing the Journey of Recovery

The small whiteboard positioned beside my bed carried my daily schedule. It remained constant during the three months I spent at ProVita.

My days were as follows: Monday to Friday, the days begun between 5 and 6 am. I was a morning person, especially since I started running more. In Abu Dhabi, during most of the year, before or after sunrise is the best time for outdoor exercises. At 9 am, I had physiotherapy sessions with Metha. It targeted my lower body for strength and mobility restoration.

Metha and I have cultivated a strong bond, growing our relationship day by day. We began as therapist and patient when I entered ProVita, but by the time I left, we had become true friends. I will always cherish the countless conversations we had about stroke recovery, whether discussing Brunnstrom's seven stages of stroke recovery or the book he recommended I read. Even after my time at ProVita came to an end, Metha's support did not waver. He remains a constant source of guidance and care, always there to lend a helping hand whenever I need it. He genuinely cares about my well-being, and I am grateful to have him by my side on this journey.

After the session, until I was not able to walk, I would go back to the room with the wheelchair pushed by the nurses. While regaining control over my walk, I transitioned to walking with the support of a cane, until I was finally able to walk with my own legs without support or help.

Then every day, I challenged myself by taking the stairs to my room. A refreshing shower followed when my parents arrived to visit. The clinic allowed flexibility in visitor numbers and timing. Between the shower and lunch, I had a quick snack of bread with jam and an Italian coffee prepared by my parents. During their six-month stay in Abu Dhabi, they lived in my rented apartment. After, I would read my work email, although my boss and close friends advised me not to do that.

I would watch some TV or try to read a book. Holding a book and flipping pages proved to be challenging with only one hand. Later, to overcome this obstacle, I started reading electronic books using my Kindle.

Around 1 pm, it was time for lunch, prepared to support my recovery. Sometimes, my mom would even supplement it with delicious Italian dishes. I inherited my cooking skills from my mom and my grandmother, who was an amazing chef. She used to prepare delightful Sunday lunches for the entire family. The lunch had to start at 12 pm sharp, signaled by the radio broadcasting the local news. It was like the sound of a pistol used to start a race or the call for lunch for an Italian military. Later, I experienced the expression, "Eating like during the compulsory Military Service." It was when I enrolled in the Italian Military Service. After completing high school, I served for one year between October 1996 and October 1997. I did three months of basic military training. Then I was posted to Rome, my city, to serve as a personal driver and office assistant to an Air Force General.

I fed myself, except for times when I needed my mom's help with the use of a knife.

But many other patients required help from nurses for feeding. This meant that when it was time for my afternoon therapy session, there were no nurses available. Since I wore a brace on my right foot, the nurses were responsible for fitting and tying my shoes.

At 2 pm, I participated in occupational therapy with JD. In the company of JD, I have never experienced the same connection and affinity that I felt with Metha. Our bond was different, and I did not click with JD in the same way. JD and I shared a friendly and amicable relationship, but it did not quite evolve into the deep friendship I developed with Metha during my time at ProVita.

We focused on improving my hand and shoulder functions. We started with warm-up and stretching exercises, followed by coordination exercises. Then we moved on to strength exercises for the shoulder and arm. JD would say, "We need to wake up the dragon." It referred to my triceps during arm flexion and extension exercises. We usually ended the session with exercises targeting my right hand. The aim was to restore finger and wrist movements and control.

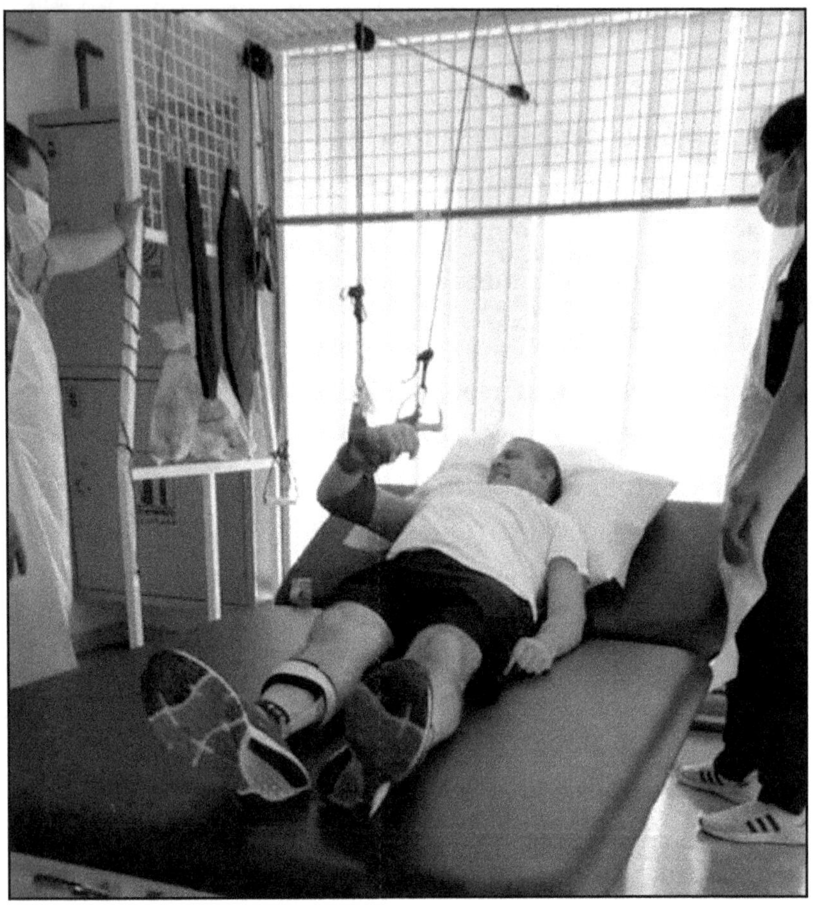

Figure 15- Marco Engaged in Arm Exercises with JD

After the therapy, I allowed myself some rest in the room. It was time to recharge and reflect on the progress I made. I filled the time before the afternoon visiting hours with chatting with my parents. Besides, I would scan the Internet for new techniques to help my recovery. I would read about stroke rehabilitation. I always enjoyed learning new subjects. And this time with stroke recovery was not different. Like when I started learning coding in Python to manage tabular data.

During the afternoon, I often received visits from friends and colleagues. They provided emotional support and motivation throughout my rehabilitation journey. As the evening approached, dinner was served at 7 pm. Afterward, I enjoyed some leisure time. It included watching television or reading. Around 11 pm or midnight, it was time to settle down for the night. I longed for a restful sleep for my body and mind for the challenges and progress of the following day.

The weekend brought a noticeable shift in my schedule. I had a different routine. There was only one therapy session scheduled for Saturday. No sessions on Sunday. The atmosphere was filled with a sense of autonomy and self-guidance. Yet, the absence of structured therapy left me wondering how to fill the void. Metha came to the rescue with a thoughtful solution. He recognized the importance of maintaining progress and momentum. Thus, Metha provided me with a stationary bike. I was determined to make the most of this opportunity for self-directed therapy. I had the freedom to experiment with different exercises on the stationary bikes.

The highlight of the weekend was the Saturday lunch prepared by Masoud's wife, Sophie. A dear friend who had opened her kitchen to create culinary masterpieces for us. It was evident that the chef prepared the food with care. The flavors danced on our tongues. A symphony of spices, herbs, and textures that created a memorable dining experience. The dishes displayed her cultural roots and her cooking skills. Sophie's dishes were a culinary marvel, captivating both the senses and the palate. She delighted us with dishes that could rival those found in Michelin-starred restaurants. From lovely shrimps to succulent grilled fish, vibrant salads bursting with freshness, and the rich flavors of butter chicken.

The portions were generous in size. As such, we made a conscious effort to leave some food for dinner. And, if possible, even for Sunday lunch.

Routine for her, preparing lunch held little significance. Yet, to me, it meant so much more. They made my weekend special.

The weekends attracted a larger group of visitors, including friends and colleagues. They took the time to visit me. Teammates also appeared during the weekend. Their visits bridged the gap between work and personal life. They reinforced the notion that our connections extend beyond the office walls. Their presence filled the room with warmth and support. They made the weekend even more vibrant and uplifting. As visitors crossed the door, their smiles radiated genuine care and encouragement. We shared laughter, stories, and reminisced about shared experiences. It allowed me to escape my rehabilitation program and immerse myself in cherished memories.

Old Habits, New Tricks

During my time at ProVita, I underwent a transformative journey. The rehabilitation program gave me back an independent life. I relearned old habits using new tricks. Once taken for granted, they became precious milestones on my path to recovery. From the simplest acts of tying my shoelaces and brushing my teeth to the more intricate tasks. These are the reclaimed habits. They symbolized the spirit that emerged during my time at ProVita:

- At the hospital, I wore an adult diaper and a urinary catheter. At ProVita, they helped me by using a comodo chair. It provided comfort and was easy to use. Then, they helped me in controlling my bladder and bowel movements. They monitored and documented my continence patterns. They offered advice and education to promote continence while preventing complications.
- They assisted me with personal hygiene. They ensured a safe and clean environment. They helped me maintain my privacy and dignity throughout the process. We transitioned from using wipes to showering with the help of a comodo chair. Later, they instructed me how to shower with one hand. They provided adaptive techniques and tools like a brush with a long handle. We went even further. I adapted to shaving and brushing my teeth with my left hand.
- It was difficult using my non-dominant hand. Early

on, the nurses provided support with feeding. The nurses assisted me in positioning myself for meals. They prepared and cut food into manageable portions. They helped with utensils and adaptive devices to ease one-handed feeding. They guided and encouraged me throughout the process. They allowed me to regain independence in feeding myself over time.

- They knew the importance of regaining my independence. Thus, they taught me techniques to perform daily activities with using one hand. My non-dominant hand. They demonstrated and guided me through tasks such as eating and dressing. They helped me develop new strategies and adapt to my changed abilities. They taught me how to dress and undress with one hand. They guided me through each step, breaking down the process in small stages. I learned that I could not dress and undress standing, but only seated. Among all actions, undressing was the activity demanding the greatest number of energy spoons from my daily reserve.
- Their expertise empowered me to regain confidence and adapt to my changed abilities. I could perform the daily activities with increased independence. As an example, I learnt to scratch myself at every possible corner like a bear with a tree trunk.
- I acquired the skill of sleeping on one side, adapting to my body's needs. I also mastered the art of getting

in and out of bed without complications. I learned the importance of mindful positioning while sleeping. I discovered the need to be conscious of my right arm's position. I had to ensure it did not stay behind my body to prevent complications. This awareness became a valuable practice. It promoted a restful and healing sleep.

- I trained in the art of falling and getting up from the ground. This practice instilled in me a sense of resilience. It reduced the fear of potential accidents. I gained confidence in my ability to navigate unexpected situations.
- I learned to operate my mobile phone with my left hand. I utilized any available object for support. I practiced typing on my laptop using only my left hand, preparing for my eventual return to work.
- I tried to learn writing with my left hand. I exercised with capital letters and numbers of children's books. All with alternate results. The difficultly was to make a straight line. Even if only a few centimeters. I tried to do my signatures and I had better results with it.

At ProVita, everyone helped me in reclaiming my independence. Their approach resembled that of teaching me familiar habits through innovative methods. By the end, I was ready to navigate my daily life.

Figure 16- Marco embarking on the journey to learn the art of writing with his left hand.

Figure 17- Marco, with Metha and JD,
cautiously rediscovering social life, explores a mall.

MY FIRST STEPS

I am walking again! my heart erupted.

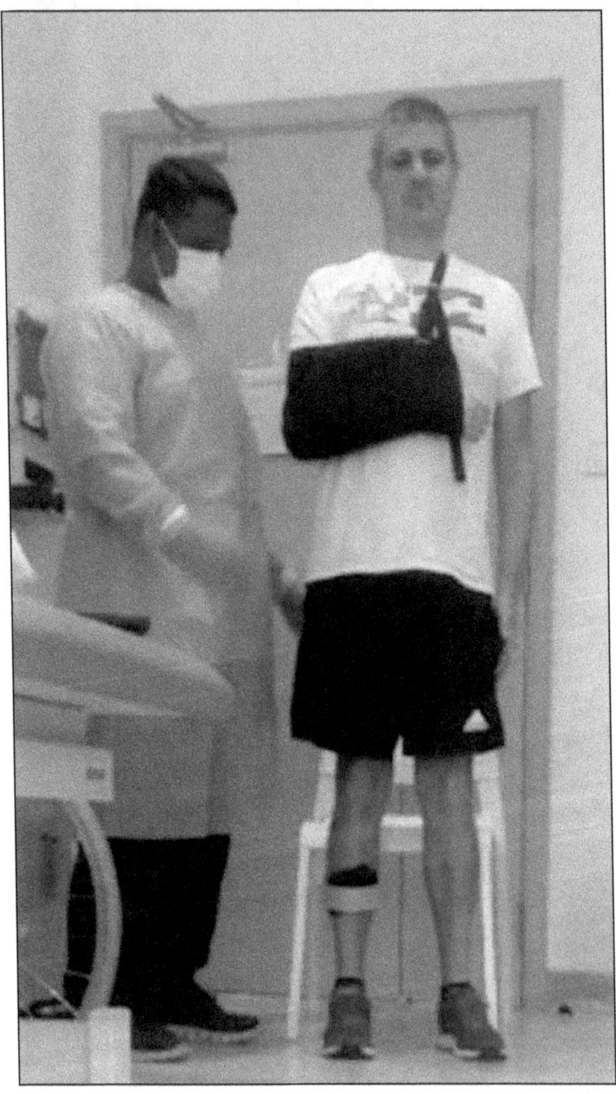

Figure 18- Marco is ready to take his first unassisted steps.

My rehabilitation journey commenced with a focus on building strength and endurance, beginning with sitting in a wheelchair. The goal was to regain the ability to endure extended periods of sitting, starting with a manageable time limit of up to one hour per day. With each session, we worked, pushing the boundaries of comfort, and increasing the duration.

Metha and I agreed that in preparation to try to walk again, the initial training sessions would include exercises focusing on a range of motion movements to prevent muscle stiffness and joint contractures. We targeted specific exercises such as flexing and extending the limbs, rotating the joints, and performing gentle stretches. All these movements help with increasing blood circulation, maintaining joint mobility, and preventing muscle atrophy. Additionally, balance exercises were incorporated to enhance my stability and coordination. I was encouraged to perform weight shifts while seated and standing, practicing reaching in different directions while maintaining balance. These exercises aimed to improve proprioception, body awareness, and overall stability.

We went through a bit of theory, by reviewing the mechanic of proper walk gait. During a normal walking gait, hip flexion occurs as the leg swings forward. This movement involves bending the hip joint, lifting the thigh, and bringing the knee toward the chest. As the leg moves forward, the foot clears the ground. This clearance is necessary to prevent tripping or stumbling, ensuring a smooth and safe walking motion. The amount of hip flexion and foot clearance can vary, depending on factors such as walking speed, individual gait patterns, and environmental conditions.

With the assistance of the nurses and under the guidance of therapists, I embarked on the challenging journey of taking a few steps around the room. My right leg, rigid as a metal bar, because the stroke gifted me an abnormal increase in muscle tone that led to spasticity where my muscle contractions become intense and involuntary, posed a formidable obstacle, making each step arduous and nearly painful. Despite the difficulty and discomfort, I remained determined, knowing that each step brought me closer to regaining my mobility and the freedom to walk independently once again. In addition to my stiff right leg, another challenge arose with my foot refusing to stay flat while walking. My foot had a deformity called "**equinovarus**." My foot was contracted and twisted inwards. The outside border of the foot was in contact with the ground and not the bottom of the foot. This made balancing difficult, combined with difficulty clearing the ground when swinging the leg through each step. This presented yet another hurdle to overcome before being able to walk again.

Besides spasticity and **equinovarus** foot, I had drop foot or foot drop (medically known as peroneal nerve injury). It is a common walking challenge caused by stroke. People with drop foot cannot raise the front part of the foot because of weakness or paralysis of the muscle that normally lifts it. With foot drop there is difficulty "clearing" the foot while walking, often dragging, or scuffing along the ground. Foot drop can result in poor positioning and unsteadiness of the ankle and knee while standing. Balance problems are common. People commonly compensate by adjusting the way they walk. One of the common compensations is called "circumduction gait." I also adopted this classic compensatory pattern to gain foot clearance called. In the circumduction gait, the hip is abducted, and the leg remains straight and swings to the side in a semicircle to move forward. The results are slower walking, fatigue over short distances, higher energy use, and possibly lots of falling. To address the issues with my foot's unnatural position and counter the compensatory patterns, the doctor prescribed a brace for me to wear. This specialized device provided the necessary support and stability, helping to align my foot correctly while walking. With the brace securely in place, I could feel its gentle guidance assisting my foot in maintaining a proper position, reducing discomfort, and ultimately regaining a more fluid and natural gait.

Following the initial standing exercises, my rehabilitation program progressed towards preparing me for walking. This involved a series of targeted leg exercises designed to strengthen and improve coordination. I engaged in leg raises, practicing lifting each leg independently. Forward, backward, and side steps were incorporated to enhance balance and stability. Additionally, bending exercises and controlled jumps were introduced to further develop strength and flexibility. Each exercise aimed to gradually prepare my legs for the intricate movements involved in walking.

Just a few days before reaching the one-month milestone since my stroke, a remarkable breakthrough occurred—I took my first independent steps. On the morning of October 4th, in the gym, I stood from the wheelchair, feeling a mix of excitement and apprehension. Metha and the assistant were by my side, their hands poised to catch me, resembling professional goalkeepers safeguarding a net. I wobbled on the verge of stumbling, yet a resolute determination fueled my every step. And finally, I was again walking solely on my own legs, marking an unforgettable milestone in my personal triumph over adversity. At that moment, my walk resembled that of a toddler taking their first steps: unsteady, wobbly, and uncertain. Nevertheless, after that significant first walk, I was ready to bid farewell to the wheelchair as my primary mode of transportation. I would walk to every therapy session and back to my room. When walking with Metha, we would take a longer route to walk on different surfaces to train my stability and balance. With each step, I grew more confident. I persisted in training, determined to adjust the adopted compensatory patterns.

I also trained doing a high knee walk resembling a marching band, accentuated by synchronized arm swing. However, due to persistent spasticity, my right arm encountered difficulty in achieving proper swing, impeding the desired walking style. This issue hindered the once harmonious coordination of arm and leg movements. Despite efforts, the spasticity-related limitation continues to persist to these days, posing a challenge in attaining the desired walk.

Walking up and down the ramps outside the villas became a regular practice, challenging my balance and coordination. The effort required to walk up the ramp felt comparable to the exertion I experienced during a long run prior to the stroke. It was during those times that I first encountered the phenomenon known as neurological fatigue. Neurological fatigue refers to a type of fatigue that affects the central nervous system, leading to a decrease in physical and cognitive performance. This condition can impact various aspects of daily activities, making them more demanding. Researching on neurological fatigue, I stumbled upon the "spoon theory." It is a metaphor often used to explain the limited energy that individuals with chronic illnesses or disabilities have available for daily tasks. According to the spoon theory, a person's energy can be represented by spoons. Each activity or task requires a certain number of spoons. Once the spoons are used up, the person may not have enough energy to continue with other activities. It is a way of illustrating the limited capacity for physical or mental exertion that individuals with chronic conditions face every day.

I also came to realize that fatigue and pain were the body's way of communicating its condition to me. I learned to pay close attention to these signals and adjust my approach accordingly. When I felt tired or encountered pain, I understood that it was necessary to halt the exercise in which I was engaged. As JD often emphasized, the "no pain, no gain" approach was not suitable, particularly in the context of stroke recovery. It was detrimental to the recovery.

With determination, I began incorporating stairs into my daily routine. Initially, I started with the technique called step-ups. It involves using a single step or platform repeatedly, lifting one foot onto the step, and then bringing the other foot up before repeating the process. As the days passed, I progressed to train with regular steps or continuous steps. This gradual approach allowed me to adapt and improve my ability to navigate stairs, ultimately enhancing my overall mobility and endurance. To this day, ascending and descending stairs are still part of my daily training regimen. I have integrated it even at work. I opted to use the stairs to reach the upper floor where my friends, Masoud and Ashraf, are located.

Each day since my first walk, I have kept visualizing myself walking confidently, feeling the ground beneath my feet, and moving with grace and fluidity. Today, after weeks turned into months since my stroke, I continue to walk autonomously, a testament to my resilience and perseverance. I have finally removed the foot brace and almost completely shed the remnants of my toddler-like walk. Those initial awkward strides have transformed into more controlled and secure strides. While my current strides have improved, they still differ significantly from a typical, graceful walk. Despite my efforts to control my right foot, it continues to slump to the ground, resembling the actions of a pizza maker working with fresh dough. It causes vibrations that travel from the foot through my leg to the rest of my body.

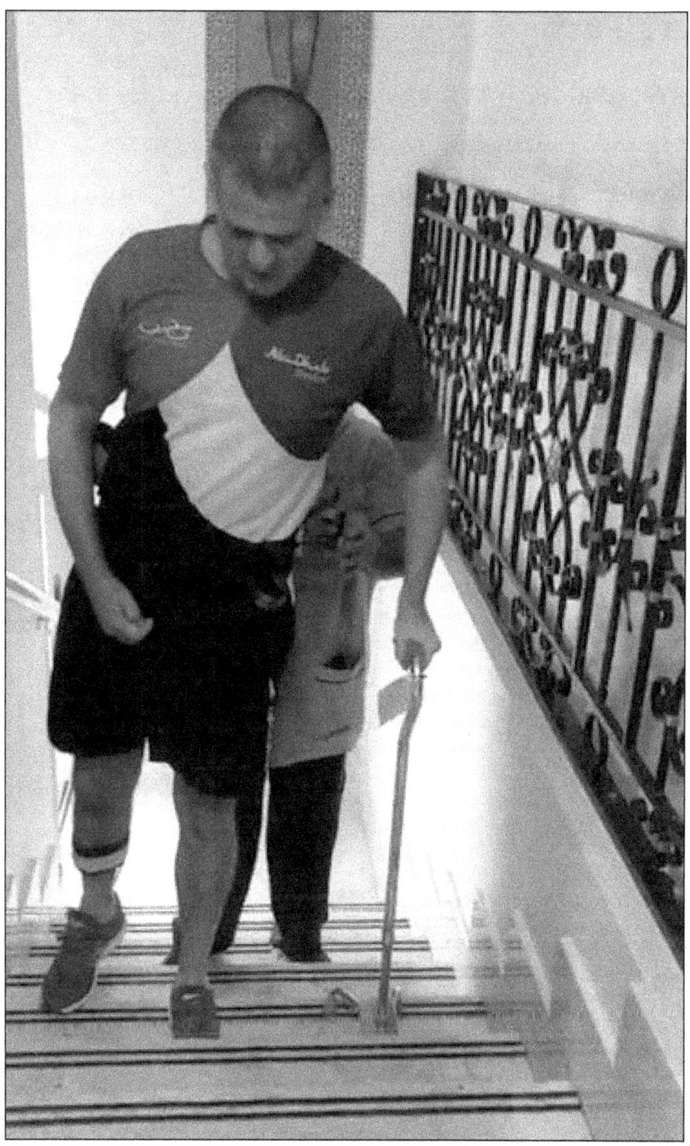

Figure 19- Marco tackling the challenge of climbing stairs using a cane.

LIGHT TROT

"My first goal is to run again within one year!" I expressed to Metha. As such, Metha selected a variety of exercises to enhance my walking training to prepare me to run again. These exercises focused on building strength, improving flexibility, and enhancing fitness.

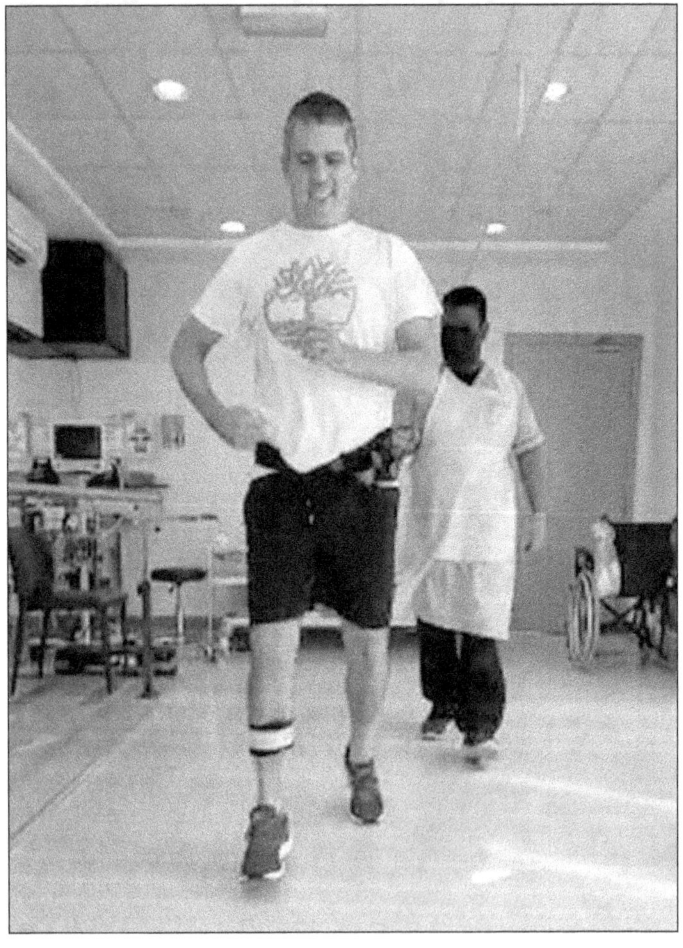

Figure 20- Marco during his first light trot alongside Metha.

One of the key exercises Metha included was squats. Squats are excellent for strengthening the lower body, particularly quadriceps, hamstrings, and glutes. Squats also engage core muscles for stability and balance. Lunges was another valuable exercise included in my training program. They work muscles in the lower body, such as the quadriceps, hamstrings, glutes, and calves. They improve balance, stability, and single-leg strength, which are essential for running. I incorporated lunges, such as walking lunges or reverse lunges. Additionally, I practiced jumping exercises. They play an essential role in developing explosive power and leg strength, thus improving running performance. In the gym, I was doing jump squats and continuous jumps like a hare. I was also jumping in the sand. The soft surface engages more muscles and increases the difficulty level.

To target my knee and hip flexors, Metha incorporated exercises like knee and hip flexions. They improve the flexibility of these joints. They allow for smoother and more efficient running movements. They also contribute to injury prevention and joint health. Additionally, Metha introduced an aerobic step as part of my training routine, which I used for various exercises, including step-ups, step jumps, or lateral movements. These exercises help enhance your cardiovascular endurance, leg strength, and coordination. Furthermore, I used the step to train one leg standing. While I had no issues standing on my left leg, standing on my right leg proved to be another story. Without relying on support, I could last only a few seconds. We also integrated treadmill walks at different speeds and inclines. Furthermore, Metha added other variations and modifications to the exercises to further challenge my muscles and add variety to my workouts.

When I made my first attempt to jog, I felt a mix of excitement and nervousness. I did the first trials in the gym before venturing outside. With Metha, we reviewed the proper gait for running in comparison to walking. During a normal walking gait, hip flexion occurs as the leg swings forward. The amount of hip flexion is smaller compared to running. The foot clears the ground by a small margin to maintain balance and cut tripping. In contrast, during running, there is a greater degree of hip flexion. The leg swings forward with increased power. This results in higher knee lift and greater foot clearance off the ground. This allows for a more dynamic and efficient stride. It helps with faster movement and longer strides. Hip flexion and foot clearance vary due to speed, and individual biomechanics. Additionally, various factors like terrain, footwear, and fatigue influence these movements.

Armed with instructions from Metha, my goal was to focus on clearing the ground with my right foot. Yet, as soon as I took a few strides and attempted to jog, I encountered an unexpected challenge. It felt as if a mysterious force pulled my right foot towards the ground, resulting in scuffing. When I propelled myself forward, my right foot seemed attracted to the surface beneath me. This unforeseen obstacle disrupted my stride and hindered my jogging. To compound matters, my right arm was stiff and rigid. Instead of assisting in my jogging efforts, it refused to move. I persevered through these initial stumbling blocks. I needed to retrain my right foot to break free from its magnetized pull towards the ground.

With each attempt, I focused on maintaining a relaxed posture. Mindful of my right foot's tendency to scuff, I tried to lift it off the ground with a determined effort. I visualized the motion. My foot gliding through the air, independent of any force like I had done a month earlier. During my initial attempts at jogging, I faced inconsistency. At times, I managed to jog without scuffing, while other times, I struggled with dragging my right foot. I needed to improve my technique for a more fluid and efficient jogging experience. I continued training in foot clearance, knowing that the root causes were hip and knee flexion.

Then, the time came to attempt jogging outside on the synthetic grass. We hoped that in this environment, I would not encounter the same issue of dragging my foot. It was a delightful sunny day in the garden, with a refreshing breeze blowing towards me. With Metha, I revisited the proper jogging gait, listening and visualizing each step. It felt as if I was already running, almost soaring through the air. With a deep breath, I began jogging, but it felt more like a brisk walk than a full-fledged jog. I remained aware that every few steps without dragging led to dragging a few more.

As the days turned into weeks, my persistence and dedication started to pay off. I was training on a 10m circle in the garden, and I completed one lap with no dragging or scuffing. A profound sense of accomplishment overwhelmed me. It was like I had reached the summit of the tallest mountain I had ever climbed. I was so excited about my achievement. I felt an exhilarating sensation, like a colt's first trot on an open plain. Uncontrolled joy surged through me.

It did not last long! During the sessions that followed, the dragging and scuffing reappeared harder than ever.

Determined, I kept training and jogging every day during my time in ProVita. But the results and emotions were often mixed. When I could not complete a lap without dragging my right foot, a sense of sadness would capture me. It felt as if I had withdrawn from a race, unable to meet my own expectations.

Even after I left ProVita, I remained committed to training and continued my attempts at jogging. Nonetheless, the frustrating reality persisted, with foot dragging hindering my progress. Despite my efforts, I could not overcome this challenge. Today, I made the decision to let go of my dream to run by the end of 2023. Instead, I have set the goal of a slow jog by that same date.

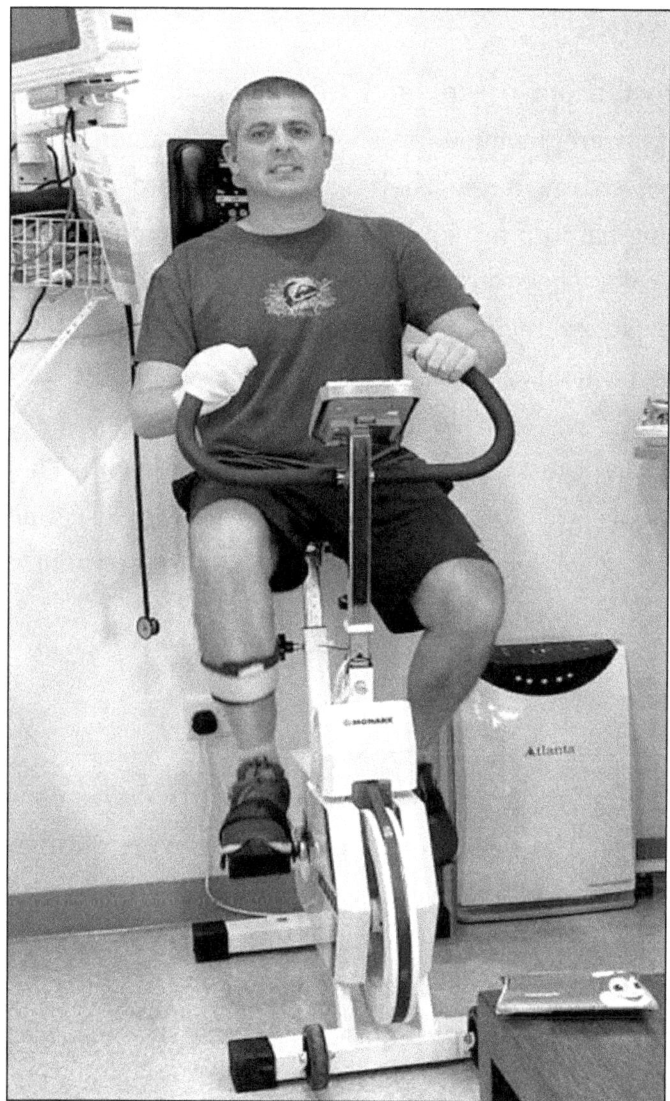

Figure 21- Marco on the static bike. He used a bandage to secure his right hand to the handlebars.

VISITORS

The visits from friends and workmates during my stay at ProVita were invaluable. They brought immense joy and comfort to my days. Their supportive words were like a soothing balm to my soul. These visits were more than mere social calls. They were pillars of motivation. They encouraged me to persevere in my recovery without hesitation. I will always remember these moments. Their support gave me strength. I was not alone in this challenging process. Their visits were a testament to the power of friendship. They had a transformative effect on my healing journey. I cannot fail to give a special mention to a few events that I remember the most.

***

Tasting "Fin'dom"

Remaining confined for an extended duration poses difficulties. The psychologist suggested having outings with friends because I was feeling lonely. Thus, there was no better way than by organizing a lunch at a fish restaurant in the vibrant Mina Port of Abu Dhabi. I went with Lei, my parents, my sister, my friends; Emmanuel, his wife, Isabelle, Laurent, and Yousef. This group of individuals represented a blend of family and close friends. They all had a significant role in my recovery journey.

Reem gathered the necessary approvals required, but they placed two conditions. One of the conditions required that a nurse go with me to ensure that they addressed all my needs as required. Another condition was to prove my ability to sit and get out of the car. JD, the therapist who guided me through my recovery process, conducted the training. We performed it in the inner space of ProVita. JD explained the importance of proper technique while sitting and getting out of a car. We discussed the challenges I could encounter. JD stated that a familiar setting would have helped me with building confidence. It would have allowed me to transfer the skills learned to real-life situations.

Next, JD explained that there are two possible techniques for sitting and getting out of a car. He then demonstrated both methods and allowed me to decide which one I wanted to use. I observed the movements and proper sequencing involved. JD emphasized the importance of using my legs and core muscles during the process. It was my time to try it. I grew confident, and I refined my technique. After several attempts, I was confident with my ability to sit and get out of the car. JD agreed that I had met the criteria to go out with my friends. I could navigate car journeys with reduced risk and increased independence.

The sun rose on a blissful Saturday morning. I started preparing for the pickup at 11:30 am with my friends, Emmanuel, and Isabelle. Mina Fish Market was a haven for seafood enthusiasts, drawing visitors from all walks of life. As soon as we arrived at the car park, the refreshing sea breeze greeted us. The aroma of grilled fish grew stronger with each step we took toward the fish market.

We made our way deeper into the fish market. The market was a bustling maze of stalls, each full of an array of seafood delights. The voices of vendors filled the air with the virtues of their offerings, while customers looked for the freshest catches. Amidst the lively chaos, we began our quest to find the restaurant suggested by Yousef. We walked in front of a line of restaurants. Finally, we reached our destination—a picturesque fish restaurant tucked away in a corner of the market. Its rustic facade and the aroma fanning from its doors beckoned us inside.

As we entered the restaurant, a friendly host with a warm smile welcomed us. The interior was cozy with nautical-themed decor that transported us to the heart of the sea. Seated at our table, we perused the menu, which displayed a wide range of seafood delicacies. From classic grilled fish to extravagant seafood platters, the choices were many. We decided on a seafood platter. It had grilled hamour (grouper fish), spicy shrimps, and garlic buttered lobster tails. While waiting, we raised our non-alcoholic drinks to celebrate the occasion. The voices from the neighboring table harmonized with ours like in an orchestra.

While eating the delicious fish, we laughed at old stories. The waiter presented the bill. I settled it, expressing gratitude for the lunch—the first outing since my arrival at ProVita. Before I left ProVita, I enjoyed other lunches with friends.

Figure 22- Stepping out of ProVita on a weekend for lunch.

***

Cake

My teammates were crucial in boosting my spirits. Their regular visits filled the clinic with warmth and laughter. Two months had passed since I entered the rehabilitation clinic. It was a significant milestone worth celebrating. My teammates decided to surprise me with a special celebration. It was a testament to their thoughtfulness and the bond we had forged during our time together.

Reem kindly allowed us to cut the celebratory cake in the clinic garden. The garden was a serene setting for our gathering. We adhered to the necessary social distancing guidelines mandated by the COVID-19 restrictions.

We realized the importance of this moment and we captured it through photographs. These visual mementos would serve as a reminder of my progress, and the bond we shared as a team. Additionally, I recorded a heartfelt message, expressing my gratitude to the entire office.

We shared laughter, stories, and conversations that further strengthened our bond. Amidst the cake cutting, we reflected on how two months had passed since we were all together at the office. It brought a sense of nostalgia. It reminded us of the shared experiences, growth, and achievements we had experienced as a team. As the cake bits disappeared, and our smiles remained, I felt a renewed sense of optimism and strength. This occasion reminded me of the power of friendship. My teammates' visits were a beacon of support and encouragement.

Their support continued to be a constant presence in my life. From the hospital to ProVita and beyond, they stood by my side, offering encouragement and strength. Even in the workplace, their constant backing became a source of inspiration and comfort.

Figure 23- The office team visiting Marco at ProVita.

***

Slices of Support: Friends Always Deliver, Just Like Pizza

Friendship is like a warm, cheesy slice of pizza that never fails to deliver support and comfort. Like a delicious pizza, true friends are there in good times and bad. They are ready to share laughter and provide a comforting presence. They bring familiarity and joy to our lives. We are not alone. Friends are the reliable slices that feed our souls and make life enjoyable. These are a few slices of memories that bring me immense pleasure when I recall them.

***

Omani Style

Masoud had been a constant presence in my life since I entered the hospital and after that in ProVita. He visited me almost every day. He offered his support and brotherhood during my recovery from the stroke. Masoud listened to my concerns and complaints. He always had words of encouragement and support. He possessed a unique ability to uplift my spirits whenever I was feeling down. He had a way of tempering my expectations. He could provide me with a realistic perspective on my situation.

Yet, one day he surprised me with an unexpected guest, his brother, Abdulla. He had traveled all the way from Oman to pay me a visit. Accompanying him were his two sons, creating a lively atmosphere in my humble abode.

The sight of Abdulla brought back fond memories of the unforgettable weekend we had spent together in Oman a few years prior. We reminisced about those days spent at the beach. We had made camp near a clear and mesmerizing sea. During that trip, I had taken up the role of the "Naked Chef," preparing breakfast while draped only in a towel. It earned me the playful nickname, one that still brings a smile to my face.

I experienced the friendly Omani hospitality. Masoud's family had welcomed me and Emmanuel into their home. They made us feel like cherished members of our own family. Their gentleness and kindness left an indelible impression on my heart.

We had always talked about returning to Oman, but time constraints have hindered our plans thus far. Everyone is caught up in the hectic whirlwind of work and family commitments, making it challenging to carve out the necessary time. Nonetheless, the memories of that camping experience in Oman remain etched in my mind. They are a reminder of the joy and camaraderie we shared.

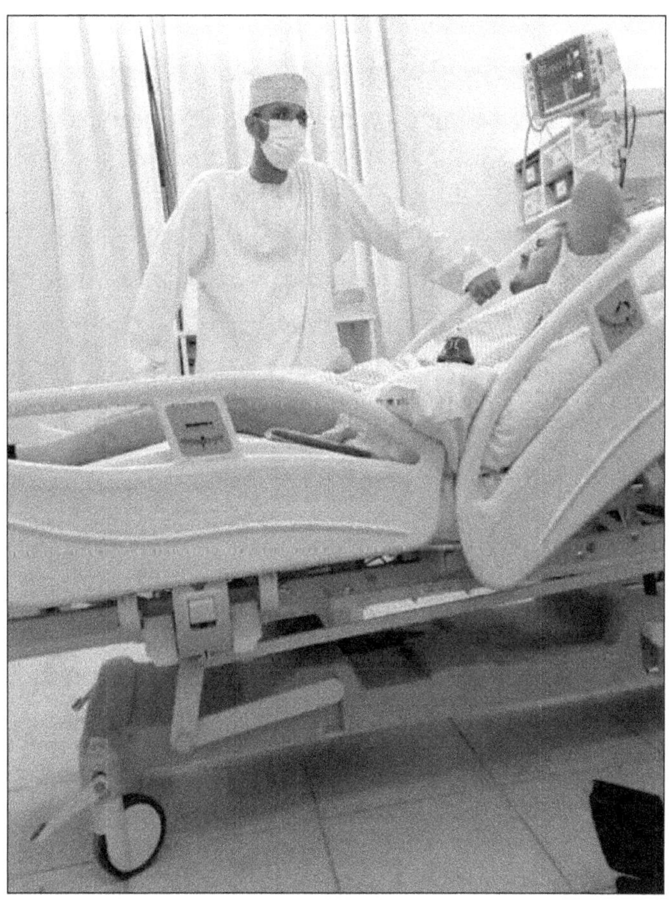

Figure 24- Marco engaging in a conversation with Masoud.

***

French Style

Emmanuel, affectionately known as Manou in my circle, and Isabelle have always been great friends to me and Lei. With Emmanuel, I shared long runs in the past. We planned to run the Abu Dhabi Marathon in December 2022 together, but for obvious reasons, I was not able to run it. We spent many afternoon and evenings on their balcony admiring the sea while tasting some good Italian food I had prepared. Unfortunately, he could not visit me as consistently as Masoud did. He commuted long distances each day. Hence, he would visit me on the weekends.

A few times, with Emmanuel and Isabelle, we enjoyed pizza in the garden of ProVita. One time, we had pizza delivered to ProVita. On another occasion, they surprised me by bringing the pizza themselves. It was authentic Italian pizza. The aroma of baked dough and the tempting toppings filled the air. Each bite transported us back to the times when I prepared pizza for everyone.

We talked about the times when we would prepare pizza together. On Saturdays, I would make the pizza dough at home, allowing it to rise for a full 24 hours. Then, on Sundays, we would gather at Emmanuel and Isabelle's house. I would take on the role of the chef, and Emmanuel became my trusty assistant. Together, we crafted delightful Roman-style Italian pizza, baked to perfection in the oven. The result was a lovely combination of a crispy bottom and a soft center. We enjoyed traditional toppings like margherita, but sometimes, we explored exotic toppings. Among the best were salad, tomatoes, shrimps or zucchini and mozzarella. We also tried Gorgonzola cheese and Italian sausages as well. They were all exceptionally tasty.

Under the shade of trees, we enjoyed the combination of great company and Italian pizza. These cherished moments reminded us of the beauty of friendship and good food.

Laurent, another dear French friend, holds a special place in my heart. Despite the demands of work and the responsibilities of caring for a newborn baby, he would be available to visit me. Laurent and his wife would share the pizza days spent on Emmanuel's balcony.

Figure 25- Marco enjoys a slice of pizza in the ProVita garden, with Lei, his mum and dad, Emmanuel, and Isabelle.

***

Italian Style

During my 10 years in the UAE, I did not have the fortune of having many Italian friends. But, when the time came, these friends rose to the occasion and provided their support. Christian, Enrico, Fabrizio, Eros, Fabio, and Andrea stood by my side. I also include Majd in the Italian family. While he is Jordanian, he studied in Italy. He also fluently speaks Italian. Christian, Enrico, Fabio, Eros, Majd, and Fabrizio were not only friends but also colleagues. Their support extends beyond personal moments, extending to the realm of work as well. Christian and Enrico would take turns to drive me to and from work. Eros and Majd took the role of softening the day at work. We work in the same office space. Eros works on my team. I am grateful for their kindness and the bond we share, both inside and outside the workplace.

I would like to extend a heartful mention to Abdulla Mohamedsharif Foolathi Alkhoori. He embodied both Emirati heritage and an adopted Italian culture. Abdulla would visit me together with Fabrizio during my time in ProVita, and we had plans to reunite once I was discharged. Sadly, Abdulla's life came to an end at the beginning of May 2023. May Allah grant him eternal peace. He is deeply missed, and his memory will forever hold a special place in our hearts.

I shall mention my other Italian friends scattered around the world: Gianni, Giovanni, Simone, Daniel, Marco, Carlo, Fabrizio, Alessandro, and Flavio. They supported me from day one and have never stopped.

One special mention goes to the Marotta Team, comprising Corrado, Luciana, Filippo, and Bianca. During the time we spent together in Abu Dhabi, when Corrado was working with me in Etihad between 2015 and 2019, they became like a second family to me. Although they later moved back to Italy and now reside in Germany, their unwavering support remained constant, especially after I had the stroke. In July 2023, they even made a special stop in Abu Dhabi on their way to Japan for their summer holidays, just to visit and extend their love and encouragement. Their friendship and care have been a pillar of strength during my recovery journey, and I am grateful for the precious bond we share.

And I could not miss my Argentinian friend, Daniel, and Cristiano from Brazil. While they are not Italian, they think and act like Italians.

***

Rest Of The World

As a proud Italian, I must admit that exotic pizza toppings like Pineapple have never quite won me over. However, I have come to appreciate and absolutely love the unique and diverse pizza toppings that my friends from around the world bring to the table.

Kevin the Captain; Jovi the Capitana; Basky the Darts Vader; Cindy the Aussie Pilateer, Jude the Researchina; Ken the Sassy Classy with a touch of Barbie (his words, not mine); Guus the

Dutch Rower; Yousef the Fez-tastic Friend; Sam and Helen the Sprinting Educators; Fia the Nordic Runner; Martin the Champion, all fellow runners and friends, have been by my side prior, during, and after the stroke. They provided comfort when I needed it the most. I want to also mention every Abu Dhabi Strider. They always had a word of encouragement and a Kudo for my walks and training sessions loaded in Strava. They celebrated my victories, encouraging me to reach for the stars. Beyond the running track, our friendship has blossomed into something beautiful. Your friendship, laughter, and shared experiences brought joy and light into my life. The memories we had together will forever hold a special place in my heart.

I cannot help but mention my dear friend, Mira. She was a semiregular attendee of the Sunday lunches at Emmanuel's place and whenever she had the chance, she made it a point to visit me at ProVita.

One last note for Stuart and Wendy. Stuart, a colleague, and friend. Lei and I were introduced to Kevin and Jovi, and hence, to the Abu Dhabi Striders by Stuart and Wendy when they were still living in Al Reef back in 2019. On the exact road where I had my stroke three years later. They used to bring me some good French and British food and laughs, along with their friendship, when I was at ProVita.

Never Looking Back

Deep inside, I vowed to myself, *I would never return to this place again.*

As I approached my departure from ProVita, I was preparing to return home. A mixture of anticipation and a sense of accomplishment filled my days.

To go home, I had to be ready for the transition. This involved a comprehensive assessment of my physical abilities, mobility, and well-being.

A month before departing from ProVita, I stopped my antidepressant medication. I felt a sense of control over my thoughts and emotions. I believed I had overcome the grasp of depression. Little did I know that a few months down the line, those thoughts would resurface once again. Depression is like a predator. It lurks in the shadow, awaiting the perfect moment to strike.

One of the main tasks was to assess my apartment bathroom, to ensure that it was safe for me. Together with JD, we examined the layout of my bathroom, paying close attention to the bathtub. We defined the changes to put in place for my safety. We discussed how I could shower on my own. We reviewed techniques for entering and exiting the bathtub without any assistance. JD's expertise and guidance were invaluable during this process. He provided practical suggestions to make my bathroom experience more manageable.

In the following days, we practiced entering and exiting the bathtub. One of the recommendations JD made was to install grab handles in my toilet area. These handles would support and assist me in maintaining balance and stability.

Weeks before my discharge, JD proposed simulating a real-life situation. Thus, we could assess my abilities. He suggested going to a nearby small shopping mall, where I would attempt to shop at a grocery store. He wanted to be sure I had no difficulties with everyday tasks, aside from those caused by using only one hand. Additionally, we planned to have lunch at the food court, where I would order and pay for my meal, as I did before the stroke. As a first step, I prepared a short shopping list, ensuring I had everything I needed. In the days leading up to the simulation, JD and Metha reviewed each step with me. I needed to be ready to return home. The day of the simulation arrived, and a car from ProVita took us to the mall. To enter and exit the car, I used the technique I had learned for outings with friends on weekends. Once at the mall, we walked around, with JD and Metha observing to ensure I was not getting tired or experiencing any mobility issues. Then, we made our way to the grocery stores. I navigated the aisles with ease. I was able to reach items on high and low shelves without any difficulties. I was even able to manage the shopping cart on my own. When it came time to check out, I paid for my purchases as I had done countless times in the past. Afterwards, we savored a meal at the food court. It marked the successful conclusion of the exercise. JD and Metha shared their contentment with how the simulation went. I, too, felt a sense of confidence and happiness with my performance.

JD and I examined every aspect of my work to ensure there were no issues. One concern I had was logging in on my work laptop. The key combination is "CTRL+ALT+DELETE." I used it to log into my work profile. Before the stroke, I could achieve this combination using both hands. But, after the stroke, it seemed impossible with only my left hand. We explored various ideas and solutions. They included the possibility of using a finger splint. I even attempted using my right hand. But I could not press any key, despite placing my fingers on the keyboard. I felt stuck at that moment. One potential solution we considered was replacing my work laptop. The new one would have a touchscreen and a virtual keyboard. I pursued that option, but when I returned to the office, I discovered an easier solution.

I defined my new home exercise routine with Metha. It included stretching and mobilization of both the upper and lower limbs. Metha emphasized the importance of walking to prevent muscles from becoming stiff. The goal was to maintain flexibility and prevent further stiffness.

We also explored other suitable rehabilitation tools. We agreed that an electro stimulator was beneficial for training my right hand. Since we had already used it during my time at ProVita, it seemed like a natural choice to continue using it. We looked at various options available on the market. We selected one sold by a company specialized in stroke rehabilitation.

As the day of my departure approached, I showered alone. The nursing staff were available in case I needed any help, such as moving out of the shower. This was a significant milestone for me, as it marked the first time I could shower almost alone. It was a step towards reclaiming my independence and returning to a more "normal" life. With each shower, I felt a growing sense of accomplishment and confidence.

Reem booked visits with my rehabilitation doctor to the cardiologist. Furthermore, I looked for a neurological visit as well.

The day before my departure, I reflected on the transformation I had undergone. I was leaving ProVita with new skills and a sense of optimism for the future.

The night before going home, sleep eluded me. I found myself revisiting every step of my journey since the stroke. While I tried to maintain a positive outlook each day, there were moments of inner turmoil. Observing my motionless hand evoked a sense of sadness within me. The inability to perform simple tasks weighed on my spirit. Yet, I persevered, seeking solace in the progress made. I hoped that each day would bring improvements.

Leaving ProVita was bittersweet. I would be saying goodbye to the supportive community that had become like a second family to me. Yet, I was eager to reunite with loved ones and reintegrate into my familiar surroundings. I carried with me the memories of the challenges I had overcome. The friendships I had forged. Before I left ProVita, I took the time to go around to say goodbye to the staff who had cared for me during the previous three months.

On December 24th, with my father by my side like three months earlier when I entered ProVita, I went out of my room for the last time. I said goodbye to the nursing staff in Villa 7 and walked out through the exit door. It felt liberating, like escaping from a prison. The day was sunny. I also pondered my fortune, walking out of ProVita on my own two legs, mindful that there were children who would spend their entire lives in long-term care at ProVita.

The transportation was waiting for us in the parking lot outside Villa 7. I entered the car happy to go back home and we crossed the main gate, and I said goodbye to ProVita.

Figure 26- Last seconds in ProVita.

The Road to Recovery: From Rehab to Real Life

In this section, I will transition from the rehabilitation center to everyday life. It is a story of the gradual steps I had taken to reclaim a sense of normalcy. Join me as I recount the challenges faced and the milestones achieved on the road to recovery.

Home Sweet Home, Finally!!

As I entered my apartment for the first time, I was struck by a mix of familiarity and strangeness. Having grown accustomed to the look and feel of ProVita, my old space felt distinct. It felt almost foreign to me. Yet, as I stepped inside, a rush of memories flooded my mind. They transported me back through the six years I had spent in that very place.

In a matter of seconds, it was as if I were watching a vivid movie of my life in Abu Dhabi. Images flashed before my eyes. Each frame holds stories and experiences. The walls whispered tales of laughter and tears. The furniture, once merely objects, now held significance as witnesses to my journey.

I walked through each room, retracing the steps of my past self. The kitchen, where I had cooked countless meals and shared conversations with loved ones. The living room, where friends had gathered for celebrations and shared in both joyous and challenging times. The bedroom, where I had sought solace and dreams for the future.

The morning light streamed through the windows, casting a warm glow that illuminated the space. It was a familiar touch, a gentle reminder that despite the changes and the passage of time, this place was still mine. And as I stood there, enveloped in nostalgia, I realized that my apartment held the chapters of my life, a testament to the moments that had shaped me in Abu Dhabi.

On December 24th, Christmas Eve, we were invited to Kevin and Jovi's place for lunch and a Secret Santa exchange to celebrate my return. This annual event has become a cherished tradition, woven into our lives for the past few years. However, for dinner, I planned to be at home with my parents and Lei. On Christmas Day, we had invited Andre and his family, a dear friend from ProVita.

Since I left ProVita, my focus shifted towards three paramount goals: continuing my recovery, reclaiming my life, and returning to work. These objectives served as guiding lights, propelling me forward with determination and resilience. I embraced every opportunity to regain strength and functionality and sought to reintegrate into my daily routines. To reconnect with cherished activities and friends. I wanted to rebuild the sense of normalcy. Ultimately, my sight was set on resuming my work. I was eager to reestablish myself in the workplace and contribute my skills once again.

In need of a change, I also decided to move to a new apartment. In February 2023, I would move to the Al Raha area from my old place in Al Reef, which would provide me with better facilities and areas to walk for my rehabilitation. Over time, this change would prove to be beneficial for me.

Christmas At Home!!

It was Christmas Eve, a special day filled with anticipation and joy. The occasion served a dual purpose of celebration. Not only was it a day to commemorate the festive season, but it was also an opportunity to mark my return.

The time finally arrived, and we made our way to Kevin and Jovi's place. We stepped through their door. The kitchen greeted us with a symphony of delightful aromas wafting in the air. We felt hungry owing to the mouthwatering aroma of holiday dishes.

Upon entering the house, everyone greeted me and asked how I was doing. I replied to everyone with a standard monologue, stating that I was doing well and improving day by day. These were the same lines I would use when returning to work the following month.

We all gathered. Laughter and cheerful conversations echoed through the living room. The air buzzed with anticipation. We were not only going to have a delicious lunch, but we were also enjoying the tradition of Secret Santa. Excitement danced in our eyes. We all placed a wrapped gift under the Christmas tree.

A grand feast, a culinary masterpiece was on the table. Roasted turkey, glazed ham, and an array of delectable sides adorned the table. It showed the effort and love poured into every dish. The meal was a symphony of flavors, a celebration of togetherness.

The time came for the highlight of the afternoon—the Secret Santa exchange. We took turns calling out the names written on the gifts. Each package held a chosen token of appreciation and love, a reflection of the unique bond we shared. Gratitude filled the room as we kept unwrapping the gifts. We cherished the heartfelt gestures from our loved ones.

As the day ended, the warmth of friendship and the joy of the season enveloped us. The celebration strengthened our friendships. Everyone marked my return with open hearts and open arms. It was a day of connection, laughter, and love.

Unwrapping the Gifts Left Me By the Stroke

Like Santa, the stroke had bestowed upon me unexpected gifts. Leaving ProVita, I carried with me the lasting impact of the stroke. It had affected not only my physical health but also my mental well-being. The time had come to unwrap the unexpected gifts that the stroke had left behind.

I experienced weakness and spasticity in the right side of my body. Spasticity is a condition characterized by increased muscle tone and involuntary muscle contractions.

In my arm, it manifested as tightness, stiffness, and exaggerated reflexes. It was like enduring relentless muscle cramps without respite or wearing a constricting compression sleeve that refused to loosen its grip. And you can imagine its impact on fine motor tasks such as writing. The days spent at the hospital and the impact of the stroke caused the muscles on my right side to diminish in size. My leg and arm were like slender handmade fettuccine pasta strands.

Due to spasticity, my arm remained in a flexed posture. It was in a bent or contracted position without my control. This hindered the ability to extend or straighten my arm. Furthermore, my right hand was clenched. The fingers were in a constant state of tightness, making it difficult to open or relax them. My fingers resembled the pincers of a crab, resistant to releasing their grip. The muscles in my fingers protruded from my forearm. They exerted pressure and caused my wrist to remain flexed. To prevent muscle contracture, I had to release my thumb from inside the clenched hand.

This clenching impaired the functionality of my hand. It limited my ability to perform everyday tasks. To find relief, I had to stretch my arm and fingers many times throughout the day. This repetitive stretching became a necessary routine. It provided temporary relief from the persistent spasticity. It alleviated the tension and stiffness in my muscles. At work, there were days I dedicated a significant part of my time to stretching my fingers. Even to wash my hands, I had to stretch my right fingers.

The stroke left me with the challenge of being one-handed as it affected the function and mobility of my dominant hand. This change forced me to adapt and find alternative ways to perform tasks that I used to take for granted. Out of necessity, I had to adapt and become left-handed, relying on my non-dominant hand for every task.

Spasticity is a stubborn turnbuckle. With Botox and stretching, we unscrew its threads, but over time, it tightens its grip again. It pulls at our muscles, turning them tense like the cables of a bridge. But we persevere, stretching and fighting, determined to find freedom from its grip.

Having Botox injections helped my muscles to relax. Botox injections involved the administration of botulinum toxin. The doctor injected it into specific muscles. Its effect was to block the nerve signals responsible for muscle contractions. The effects of Botox injections would only last for a span of three to four months. So, I had to repeat the injections to maintain the temporary relief they provided. This cycle of repeating the injections became necessary to manage the spasticity.

Despite efforts to address it during my time at ProVita, the shoulder subluxation persisted. After I returned home, I sought help from Etihad Medical. They took action to reverse the condition. Yet, the subluxation had already taken its toll. It limited the range of motion in my arm. And it caused my elbow to swing to the side during movements.

The restricted mobility and shoulder subluxation resulted in a new posture. Like that of a bird spreading its wings, with my arm extending outwards and away from my body. The involuntary spasms in my right arm hindered my sleep. The doctors advised me to take Gabapentin and Valerian to help me sleep, which were effective only until the early hours of 3 or 4 am. Beyond that, my arm functioned as an unwelcome alarm, growing rigid and inflexible. When I laid down with my arm bent at the elbow, my fingers found their only break in straightness. Flexing my wrist granted them the ability to stretch and extend. In this position, my right hand resembled the formidable foot of a crocodile. Upon noticing my straight fingers, I thought I was going to regain their control soon. My hopes were dashed as it never became reality. So far. Or I would laugh, thinking that my straight finger resembled E.T.'s finger. A touch of magic in my own uniqueness. It took me six months to be able to turn on my right side while resting in bed.

Besides the spasticity affecting my arm, I also experienced spasticity in my right leg and foot. I had limited, almost no control over my ankle and foot. They were subject to involuntary movements and tightness. This lack of control posed challenges for walking, balance, and coordination. My right leg bore the weight of steel, hindering its movement with each step. It made each movement a considerable challenge. The heaviness I experienced added an extra layer of difficulty to overcome. Furthermore, with each step, my right knee would hyperextend or buckle, adding challenges to my walking. The issues persisted even when I stood upright. It made it difficult to maintain a stable and balanced posture. Moving in closed spaces was challenging. My walk was a crab-like dance, graceless and clumsy. At times, I found myself moving in a manner reminiscent of a "drunken Dutch walk." It was an unsteady walk that resembled the movements associated with intoxication. To move to my right and backward, I had to execute a graceful half pirouette, almost on tiptoe, like a ballerina. Showering, dressing, tying one's shoelaces, and making coffee are normal tasks for most. But to me, they posed challenges. Each action required intense focus and attention. I feared stumbling, dropping, or damaging something in the process.

I swapped the belt for suspenders and replaced trousers with an elastic band instead of a zipper and button. Instead of a buttoned shirt, I opted for a collar shirt. While I knew there was a special tool for handling buttoned shirts with one hand, I found collar shirts easier to wear. I also switched my shoelaces for elastic ones with clips, which are perfect for someone with limited hand mobility.

I could not drive. Swimming or even floating became a challenge as I struggled to maintain buoyancy. I had to confine myself to shallow waters or rely on the help of a float. I was unable to ride a bicycle, but I rode a stationary bike.

After a stroke, sensory issues manifest in various ways. They can disrupt the normal perception and processing of sensations. For example, individuals may experience excessive sensitivity to touch. When even light contact can feel painful or overwhelming. Some may suffer from decreased sensitivity. It can lead to a diminished ability to feel touch, pressure, or temperature changes. After the stroke, my arm turned to ice when exposed to cold temperatures. Spatial awareness abandoned my right limb, leaving it a stranger in my own body. It collided with walls, doors, and corners as I stumbled through the world. Every noise was a gunshot. Each touch an unexpected invasion, sending shivers down my spine. Stunned, I would leap like a protagonist in a chilling tale. My heart would race in terror. My senses conspired against me. They turned mundane moments into suspenseful scenes from a horror film. I longed for equilibrium amidst this disconcerting realm. When my heart rate increased or I started feeling stress, my arm stiffened and flexed inward. It functioned as a shield to protect me from the external world.

Owing to the weakness of the muscles in the right side of my face, I would unintentionally bite my lips. The repeated instances of this act caused me pain each time. I thought my speech was slurred, making communication difficult.

After the stroke, I stayed optimistic and positive, but depression appeared as a risk. The antidepressants had shielded me from its grasp. Yet, I knew I had to confront it sooner rather than later.

Medicals

Upon returning home, a new stream of medical visits commenced. They aimed at aiding my recovery. The journey encompassed various crucial aspects of my health. Rehabilitation became an integral part, addressing both the need for Botox injections and alleviating persistent shoulder pain. The diligent cardiologist took charge, meticulously examining my blood pressure, cholesterol levels, and blood sugar, while consistently prescribing the necessary daily medications to keep my condition in check.

Seeking further therapeutic support, I embarked on physiotherapy sessions at Etihad Medical, where Euyanna used her expertise to help me with my recovery. Her help proved invaluable in alleviating shoulder subluxation. Yet, my wrist and fingers remained reluctant to respond and cooperate. And last, but not least, a visit to the neurologist became paramount. It was an opportunity to clear up the doubts about artery dissection and blood clots. They had caused the stroke. The neurologist, Dr. Shobhit Sinha, advised me to undergo an MRI scan of my neck and head, both with and without contrast. Five months after experiencing a stroke, I found myself once again lying in the MRI machine. The anticipation among everyone involved was palpable. Questions filled my mind: "Had the blood clot disappeared? Is the dissection repaired?" They consumed my thoughts in the days leading up to the scan. Finally, the morning of the scan arrived, and I faced it with unwavering confidence. The operator began injecting the contrast liquid into my bloodstream. A metallic taste flooded my mouth. It was like the sensation of sucking on a rusty lollipop. Inside the confines of the machine, memories of the morning I entered the ER came rushing back. The same sense of apprehension and unease enveloped me. In my mind, I was reliving those moments all over again.

A few days after the scan, the doctor called me to share the results. The radiology lab had released them. To my immense relief, the artery showed no signs of dissection, and the blood clot had vanished. I happened to be at work when I received the call. Eager to absorb all the information without any distractions, I found a small couch to sit on. A wave of relief washed over me, and excitement surged through my veins. I wasted no time in sharing the incredible news with everyone around me. I wanted them to join in my joyous moment.

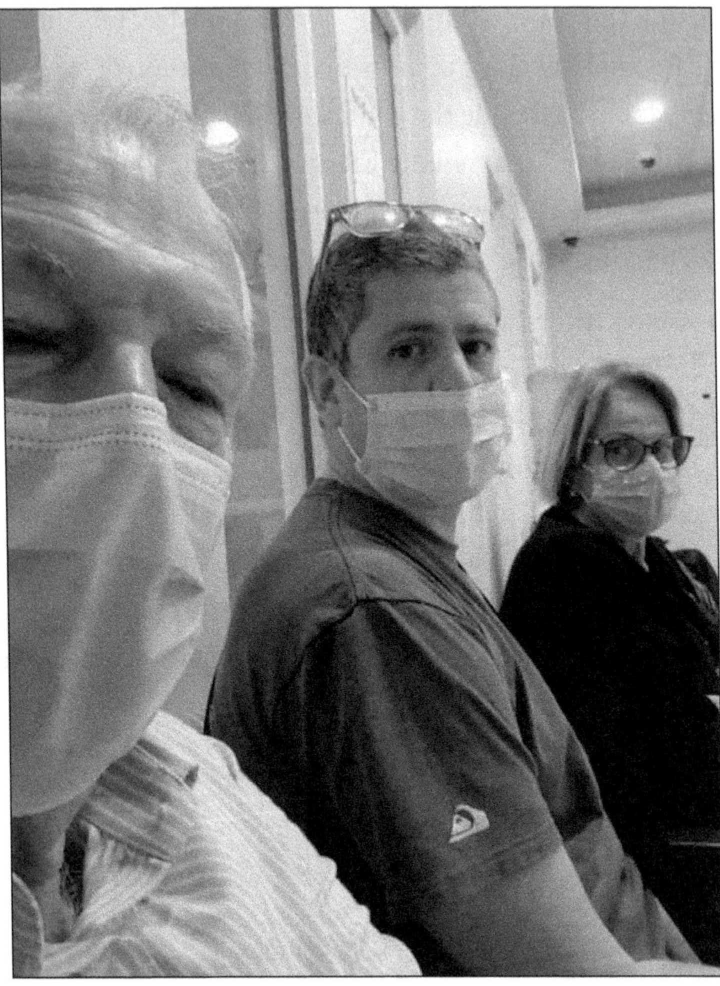

Figure 27- Anticipation building in the waiting room as Marco awaits his turn for the MRI scan.

Going Back to Work

As I stepped into the office, I whispered to myself, "I am finally back."

To return to work, I had to first get clearance from Etihad Medical. I booked an appointment with Dr. Jose Puno Villanueva, specialist in Occupational Medicine, on January 20th, 2023. It was two days before my 47th birthday. The visit was pleasant and cordial. Dr. Jose was friendly. He took the time to review my case and assess my status. He provided valuable recommendations about returning to work, particularly during emergency evacuations. He told me to stay positive because our dreams and beliefs propel us towards our goals. It was a reassuring encounter. It left me with confidence and a sense of direction as I prepared to resume my professional journey. We agreed that Monday, January 23rd, would be my first day at work. Exactly 137 days since I had the stroke.

I woke up early that morning, eager to be prepared. I had a cup of coffee, took a shower, and dressed up. I wanted to be ready for Mansoor's pickup at 9 am. Before leaving home, my father captured a photo of me. My mom wished me good luck, and I picked up my office bag. As per usual, I had prepared my work bag the evening before. I stepped outside, ready to conquer the world.

Figure 28- Marco is ready for his first day back at the office.

Mansoor had to delay our arrival because a welcome party was about to start at the office. I was the guest of honor at the welcome party. The entire office was waiting for my arrival, creating a sense of anticipation.

Stepping foot into the office after four long months since my stroke was a significant occasion, which brought with it a mixture of emotions. I was eager to begin. Yet, I questioned whether I was truly prepared for the task ahead.

The entire office had been decorated with vibrant balloons. Colorful banners with warm messages of welcome adorned the walls. It was a heartfelt gesture, a symbol of the support and love that surrounded me.

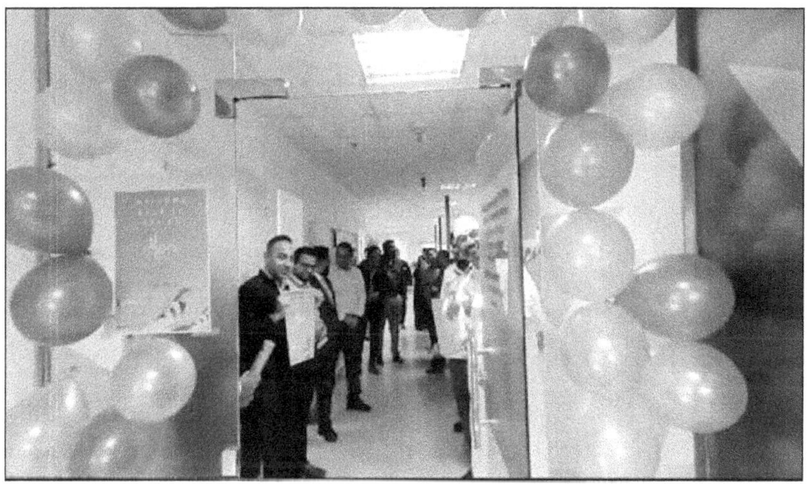

Figure 29- Marco's Triumphant Return: Stepping into the Office Post-Stroke

I slowly made my way through the office, taking in the smiles and greetings from my colleagues. They had eagerly awaited my return for months. Their eyes sparkled with genuine happiness, and their warm embraces enveloped me in a sense of belonging. I realized the true value of a supportive work environment and the bonds forged through shared experiences. It felt like my very first day at Etihad, all over again.

Figure 30- Colleague's Warm Welcome: Marco's Heartwarming Return

As my old desk had limited space, they assigned me a new desk. It was in a corner of the office, away from my old desk and my team. It provided a bigger space for me to move around and feel more comfortable. My team assisted me in arranging my new desk, connecting the laptop to the network for updates. We also configured my old office phone and arranged my screens. As I settled into my new workspace, I was met with an outpouring of kind words and encouragement. Throughout the day, colleagues approached me with sincere inquiries about my health and well-being. They were genuinely concerned. They listened intently as I shared snippets of my recovery journey. They expressed a mix of empathy, encouragement, and support. The conversations were filled with laughter, as we reminisced about shared memories and lighthearted moments, creating an atmosphere of camaraderie.

Finally, I was left alone at my desk. I felt a mix of excitement and awareness that things had changed. I was not the same person who left the office on September 7th, 2022.

I understood the need to adjust my working style to accommodate my limitations. With only my left-hand functioning. I was also worried about my speech imperfections. I struggled to complete sentences. I was of the impression that I was missing the last few words of each sentence. My mouth did not want to move properly while speaking. I spent 30 minutes staring at the screens, unsure of where to begin. I was lost, just like a new kid at school. Fortunately, my team was there to make me feel comfortable.

The day progressed, and the office buzzed with the rhythm of productivity. It was a stark contrast to the silence that had filled my days during the months of rehabilitation. It fueled my determination to reclaim my professional life, despite the challenges I had faced.

My teammates would approach my desk asking if I needed any assistance or support.

On the first day, Masoud came to see me, and there was a palpable sense of awkwardness as we crossed paths at the office. Both of us were acutely aware of it. Over the past four months, he had been a constant presence, visiting or calling almost every day. Since the day I entered the emergency room, he had never left my side. During our meeting, we delved into a discussion about my work situation and the arrangement of my office. He wanted to ensure that I was fully prepared to resume my work. During our conversation, he informed me about certain office politics. He suggested that I regain my position within the office. I had a reputation for being articulate and persuasive. People tended to listen to me and agree with my viewpoints. I possessed the ability to sell my ideas. I always emphasized the notion that "It's not just what you sell, but how you sell it that makes all the difference." In the subsequent weeks, he continued to stress the same message repeatedly.

Masoud has been my constant companion ever since I first set foot in the office. We engaged in lengthy conversations. I sought his help many times. His advice has been instrumental in shaping my journey ever since. He has proven to be a benevolent brother figure, a true pillar of strength for me.

Later that day, Rami, my boss, approached me to offer his welcome. After exchanging the customary greetings and inquiries, he reassured me of the flexibility to leave the office whenever necessary to attend medical appointments. As the months went by, Rami consistently demonstrated his openness and support for my needs. He always made sure to fulfill every request I had without hesitation. He consistently maintained an open-door management style, making himself readily available for conversations whenever I needed to speak with him.

For the first two days, I went around the office, extending greetings to everyone, whether they had visited me at the hospital or rehabilitation center or sent messages of recovery during my absence. Many individuals recounted anecdotes about their relatives or friends who had experienced strokes in the past. They shared that over time, most of them had successfully recovered. The prevailing atmosphere was one of positivity and encouragement, with everyone trying to uplift and inspire me. Whenever people inquired about my well-being and progress, I had a prepared response. I would confidently state, "Overall, I am doing well," and then express my gratitude for being alive. I would emphasize taking one step at a time, assuring them that I was on the path to recovery. Many individuals would remark that I looked better than the last time we had encountered each other. Whether it was during my time at ProVita or outside of it.

Most people were curious about my limitations and how I was coping with them. I always responded with polite answers, yet, deep inside, I wanted to scream, "What the fuck, can't you see that my right hand doesn't move?!"

During the rest of the week, I focused on figuring out my next steps. While I was away, Sudhir had taken on my responsibilities. Together, we reviewed the status of the office work. We discussed the progress of ongoing projects and those in the pipeline. Since I kept reading my work email, I did not get too many surprises.

During the first week, the Health and Safety Department from

Etihad visited me. They had received the report from the Occupational Medicine Team and wanted to ensure that I was satisfied with my office setup. They specifically inquired about how I would manage writing. I explained that most of my work was computer-based, and I was adapting by using only my left hand for typing. I mentioned that during my time at the rehabilitation center, I received training to utilize my left hand for various tasks. Furthermore, I expressed gratitude for the support provided by my teammates.

Rami went a step further and organized an official welcome party in my honor. The event also served as a celebration for the 10th work anniversary of several staff members, including me. I joined Etihad in January 2013. The first week after my return felt reminiscent of the initial week, I spent at the company a decade earlier.

Although everyone provided their support and encouragements, I want to give special recognition to a select group of individuals. They played an extraordinary role in making me feel at home.

A heartfelt thank you to Nazaif, Rohan D., Kamal, Chamini, Nelum, Marjorie, Dilip, Majd, Eros, Jacob, Qassim, and Mohamed AlFardan.

Since I went back to the office, they regarded me with familiarity. They never treated me as anything less than the person I had always been. Their kind words were a constant source of encouragement. Always ready to lend a helping hand whenever needed was nothing short of remarkable. Rohan always stretching my clenched hand. Kamal and Jacobs with their jokes and encouragements to lift my spirit up. Nazaif with his continuous help. Whether I needed a ride to the office or anything else, he was always available for me. Marjorie, Chamini, and Nelum with their prayers. Mohammed and Qassim treated me as if nothing had happened. They all fostered an environment of normalcy. During my absence, Dilip stepped up as the coffee expert in the office. Even after my return, he continued to brew, delivering one of the finest cups by a non-Italian native. Majd (Zio Jedino, uncle Jedino) and Eros (Pepperino), with their perceptive nature, uplifted my spirit, adjusting to my changing moods. Their presence in the office became a source of comfort, navigating the intricacies of my emotions. Their ability to understand and respond to my needs was a cherished gift. The time we spent talking about my sleep and rest while sipping green tea (we had established the 3 PM tea club). We found amusement in mocking and gossiping about certain colleagues in the office. We gave nicknames to the most intriguing characters, fostering a sense of shared humor. We had created our Orwellian Animal Farm. From "Topo Gigio" to "Meluccia" and "Tintin," it added a touch of levity to our office work.

Everyone supports created an atmosphere of acceptance and belonging. I will forever cherish those moments.

I would like to extend a special mention to Mr. Saidulkhadri Bin Hamzah, Senior Inspector of Aviation Safety Affairs at the UAE General Civil Aviation Authority (GCAA). Before my stroke, our relationship was professional, characterized by mutual respect and a touch of friendship. Mr. Saidulkhadri continued to visit me during my time at ProVita and maintained the same level of treatment and respect in our work interactions, not allowing my stroke to alter our dynamic.

Since my return to work, the trio known as the "three stooges" has been reunited, and the original breakfast club has once again swung its doors open. Thanks to Dilip, there is never a shortage of freshly brewed coffee. Ashraf, Masoud, and I find ourselves side by side every day. Our conversations revolve around work matters, the very book you are reading now. We delve into its cover design, its publishing process, and strategies for marketing. They never treated me with pity; to them, nothing has changed with my stroke. They are playing a significant role not only in my ongoing recovery but also in the broader spectrum of life.

Beyond the professional realm, friendships grew stronger. Breakfast and breaks became an opportunity to reconnect, to share stories and laughter. The bonds that had been forged over time had only grown deeper during my absence.

In the days and weeks that followed, my teammates continued to be my pillars of strength. They helped and gave understanding whenever I needed it, allowing me the space to ease back into my responsibilities. It was a collective effort, with everyone pitching in to ensure a smooth transition and alleviate any unnecessary stress.

With determination, I strived to reclaim the person I was

before the stroke. I understood the arduous path ahead. I acknowledged the inevitable challenges that awaited on this journey of recovery.

Looking back on that first day back at the office, I am overwhelmed with gratitude. The balloons and warm greetings were more than just decorations.

The experience of returning to the office after four months from my stroke was a testament to the power of human connection, compassion, and support. It was a reminder that setbacks are not insurmountable, and that together, we can overcome the most challenging of obstacles. As I continue to rebuild my life, I carry with me the memory of that day, a beacon of hope and strength that guides me forward.

Figure 31- 3 PM Tea Club in Full Swing, Marco (left), Eros (center) and Majd (right).

Into the Abyss: Navigating Personal Turmoil

According to medical studies, post-traumatic stress symptoms affect up to 25% of stroke survivors. Many will eventually be diagnosed with complete post-traumatic stress disorder (PTSD). Stroke-induced PTSD is linked to poor long-term stroke outcomes, increased disability, and nonadherence to pharmaceutical treatments. Similarly, post-stroke depression (PSD) affects between 18% and 33% of stroke survivors. Though the real figures could be higher.

After the stroke, I confronted various emotions that were hard to understand. This chapter provides a raw and honest account of the challenges I faced during a period of profound inner turmoil.

Since the stroke, I adopted a mindset of positivity and determination. Every day, I focused on my recovery, putting all my energies into therapy sessions and rehabilitation exercises. The thought of regaining my abilities was my driving force. Indeed, my personal distress had always been a part of me, lurking beneath the surface. However, antidepressants and my initial positivity kept those feelings at bay. They were tamed, allowing me to focus on my recovery and maintain a sense of hope. I did not know the distress was waiting for its time. It was growing stronger each day. Until it could no longer be contained.

As time went on after I left ProVita, I experienced sadness

and worry. It was like a dark cloud covering a bright and beautiful day. It felt as if I were stepping into quicksand; the harder I tried to escape, the deeper I seemed to sink. I became aware of personal distress within myself—a state of emotional or psychological discomfort experienced by an individual. Personal distress often occurs due to specific life events, conditions, or circumstances that create severe discomfort, such as interpersonal issues, financial troubles, work-related stress, or a catastrophic experience. Personal distress is shown in various ways, including melancholy, anxiety, anger, helplessness, or irritation. Emotional issues may also be accompanied by physical symptoms, such as sleep difficulties, changes in appetite, or an elevated heart rate—all of which I experienced. Personal anguish is frequently transient and may subside after addressing the underlying stressors or issues. However, when personal distress lasts for an extended period and affects everyday functioning and general health, it can progress into depression. While some emotional distress is common in life, depression comprises more chronic and severe symptoms that extend beyond transitory mood swings. As time went on, the personal distress I experienced began to morph into something deeper. It transformed into a weight that seemed impossible to shake off. The stroke manifested its impact in a profound way.

I started feeling anxious. My hands were trembling, making it hard to hold onto things. The rooms seemed to close in on me. Worries filled my head, telling me that my hand would never move again. It was like I could not escape the anxiety that was making it difficult for me to think and breathe.

I experienced episodes of unexpected and intense laughing or crying. This condition is called the pseudobulbar affect (PBA) and can affect people with neurological conditions or injuries like stroke. Sometimes, I laughed uncontrollably in response to a mildly amusing comment or situation. I would often find myself bursting into tears. I felt overwhelmed with anxiety and stress.

My job became hard. I could not do things the way I used to before the stroke. Simple tasks became overwhelming, fueling my frustration and distress. I was so scared about the future. That made everything frightening. At the same time, my personal life got influenced as well. Relationships with the people I cared for became harder. I had trouble talking. I had never imagined that one day I would find myself close to walking down the lane of depression. In contrast to my expectations, reality turned out to be different. Six months after my stroke, I started hearing the subtle melodies that depression whispered into my ear. It began as a blackout murmur. It clouded my mind and soul. That made me feel even more unsure. I could not enjoy my days or the people around me anymore. It was like the slow torture of water dripping, one drop at a time. I was getting depressed.

Like Odysseus, who was pulled in by the sirens' charming melodies, I found myself drawn to the appealing call of depression. Odysseus is the hero of the epic poem, "The

Odyssey." As Odysseus and his friends sailed near an island, they heard the sirens. These sirens had beautiful voices that could make sailors want to come closer to them. But the problem was, if the sailors got too close, they would crash their ships into dangerous rocks. To keep his friends safe, Odysseus had a clever idea. He instructed his friends to cover their ears so they would not be attracted by the sirens' songs. But Odysseus, being very curious, wanted to hear the sirens' songs himself. So, he had a different idea. He asked his friends to tie him to the ship's mast, so he could not move. His friends agreed and made sure he was secure. As the ship sailed closer to the island, the captivating voices of the sirens reached Odysseus' ears. Their enchanting melodies filled the air, tempting him to give in to their call.

Work became like climbing a big mountain that was blocking my way. I had trouble putting my thoughts into words, especially during online meetings. I struggled with completing sentences without cutting the last word or two. My right facial muscles were rigid, as if I were a robot attempting to move. It was frustrating. I could not type long emails anymore. I could only use my left hand to type. It made me uncomfortable. Sat in front of the screen, my right fingers curled like the lid of a just-opened tuna can, revealing the stiffness and tightness that gripped them. They did not want to participate as they did in the past. Helpless, they were dead bodies to me. I started looking for something to contribute to my group and the office. Coding had always been my strength, so I decided to pick up where I left off before the stroke. But my brain was foggy. I battled to find inspiration and clarity in what to do next. I could not help my team any longer. It was like going from travelling in first-class to being moved in economy class. It made me feel little and futile. I was great at my work for the previous ten years. Individuals depended on me. I was important. But that changed. I could not do things the way I used to. It made me question myself. I had lost self-esteem. Feeling futile was difficult to bargain with. A portion of me was lost. I began to address who I was and what I may contribute. It made me feel pitiful and uncertain of myself.

When I went back to work initially, people only shared stories of stroke survivors who fully recovered. But now, they started telling me about people who did not get all better after a stroke. Hearing these stories made me doubt my own recovery even more.

I appreciated driving to work and looking around me. I had a sharp eye for watching human nature. I preferred observing the individuals in other cars. Pondering around what they were doing, where they were going, and what contemplations were running through their minds. The stroke had taken away that joy as well. I had lost the flexibility of going to work and leaving at whatever hour I wanted. Before the stroke, I worked up to 12 hours a day. But after the stroke, I had to adapt my schedule to the person who was giving me a lift to work. This added even more stress to the already down feeling I had. Everything was piling up day by day. It was getting harder to cope with.

Things were not going any better in my personal life. The apparent absence of development in my recovery left me feeling discouraged. I did not observe comparable progress as I did in the initial months. I knew that most of the recovery following a stroke occurs during the initial six-month period. I hoped I was the exception to the rule. Instead of advancing in my recovery, I was staying at the same level or even going backwards. The weight of this sentiment added to the complexity of the arduous journey I was undertaking. As I stared into the mirror, all I saw were my limitations and the unexpected gifts that came with the stroke. I did not like the image I was looking at. Before the stroke, I had a fit and toned physique that I took pride in. Yet, after four months of rehabilitation, my reflection in the mirror showed a somewhat chubby version of myself. I attributed this change to the sweets from my friends and the mouthwatering pasta cooked by my mom. It seemed that indulging in those treats had taken its toll on my appearance. The gap resulting from my shoulder subluxation looked as steep as the stairs of the Spanish Square in Rome! It was like my shoulder decided to take on the challenge of being its own tourist attraction.

I longed for the power to erase the reflection in the mirror, as it served as a constant reminder of my dissatisfaction and frustration. I felt powerless. Useless. Lei had to help me with almost everything. I could not help with the house chores. She had to shower me once per week to ensure every inch of my body was clean. My skin on my left arm was developing allergic reactions because I could not thoroughly clean it. She referred helping me shower to "cleaning the rug."

The challenges I faced with moving affected our intimate moments too. I could not naturally embrace her like before. Instead, I had to awkwardly hold my right arm with my left one to create a loop of connection. It was different and took some getting used to. But we found a way to still share moments of closeness despite the physical changes.

I knew that they were problems only in my head. But these feelings were stronger than me.

Sitting on my couch, I would look at the titles of books on my shelves. Each one served as a reminder of my limitations and the things I had lost due to the stroke. One title stood out: *Training Essentials for Ultrarunning*. I purchased it a few months before the stroke, with the intention of using it to train for my upcoming 100km race. It represented my dream, my goal. But in that moment, my dream had shattered into countless pieces. One for each meter of the race I could no longer run. It was a painful reminder of the challenges I faced, and the significant changes brought upon by the stroke.

At the grocery store, I found myself constantly vigilant, carefully maneuvering to avoid colliding with others and dodging fast moving shopping carts. In my mind, all eyes were fixed on me, particularly on my motionless hand. I kept it out of sight as much as possible. Confidence diminished within me as I fought with the dilemma of greeting both friends and strangers. The customary handshake with my right hand was no longer an option. I was unsure of how to proceed. I resorted to either offering a left-handed fist bump, adhering to the old COVID-19 protocols, or awkwardly extending my right arm. It was rigid showing the stress of the situation. While some people appeared surprised by this, those who knew me well had grown accustomed to my adjusted greetings.

All these emotions had a profound impact on me, leading to a feeling of being stuck and discouraged in my recovery. I noticed that my progress was slowing down. Thus, I reduced the intensity of my exercise routine. This change also caused my willpower to decrease. I stopped appreciating who I was and what I had, focusing solely on negativity. I no longer spoke kind words of life and love to myself. Instead, I only spoke darkness and negativity. Every day, Lei would inquire about my well-being, expressing her concern with words like, "You seem sad and depressed. You are no longer finding joy in life." She was right. I could not experience happiness in life nor establish meaningful relationships with those in my surroundings. The activities that once used to entertain me now seem unfamiliar and far away like distant recollections. I had stopped reading. The smell of the ink on the paper. My fingers caressing the cover. They were all gone. Even cooking became a challenge, and I gave up. Although, in the weeks after returning home, I managed to make fresh pasta and pizza dough, using only one hand—my left one. Every evening, I would dream of my hand moving the next morning. However, each new day would bring the same lack of improvement as the day before. It was devastating. I refrained from joining my friends in the running club for walks and outings. I developed various excuses, fabricating new ones for each occasion. I had always enjoyed spending time with them. Either for a run, a walk, breakfast, or a party. But I had lost the pleasure of having fun and laughing.

Envy crept into my heart like an unwelcome guest. It attacked me when my running friends shared their race photos and stories. I was not there. I was on the sidelines. I longed to be among them, standing at the starting line. Their posts painted vivid pictures of their adventures—scenic trails, the camaraderie, the shared laughter, and triumphs. We had planned to travel together, pitching our tents under the stars. We were a tribe of runners, bound by a shared passion for pushing our limits. As I scrolled through their updates, a mix of joy for their accomplishments and a tinge of sadness washed over me. I could not help but wonder what it would feel like to cross that finish line. Running was more than a hobby; it was a part of my identity. It brought me immeasurable joy. But in that moment, it felt like a distant memory, slipping further away with each passing day.

Lei's face would light up with excitement as she swung open the door, eagerly stepping outside for her morning run. A spasm of desire stirred within me. I wanted to experience the same rush of joy.

Below my window, a symphony of pounding footsteps filled the air as runners sprinted along the canal. Just a few months ago, I would have been among them. But now, I was on the other side, gazing out from the window of my apartment. As I watched their effortless strides and the determination etched on their faces, a mix of nostalgia and longing washed over me. The vibrant energy of the runners coursed through my veins, reminding me of the freedom and exhilaration I once felt. But alas, my right leg had other plans. Its persistent tightness had become a constant companion. It did not want to leave me alone.

The stroke not only took away my ability to run, but it also stripped away the joy and experiences associated with it. The time spent with friends. The thrill of camping. The camaraderie at the starting line, and the sharing of stories and life. They were all lost.

As I passed by the roads we used to run on, an overwhelming surge of emotions washed over me. I could not help but feel a wave of sorrow deep within. Memories flooded my mind—the moments when our muscles strained with utmost effort. Beads of perspiration trickled down our bodies, eventually pooling in our soaked socks and shoes. The wet footprints we left behind on the glistening tarmac functioned as directional markers, guiding those who would follow in our running footsteps. Yet, amidst the physical discomfort, there was an undeniable sense of purpose and fulfillment. However, as I gazed upon those familiar roads, I could not shake the realization that those extraordinary sensations might forever elude me, becoming distant echoes of a time that I would never fully experience again.

Despite my usual aversion to financial risks, during that

period, I made a foolish decision that not only failed to yield the desired returns but also resulted in the loss of a portion of my life savings. I was upset with myself. It was yet another piece of the puzzle contributing to my growing sense of depression. While reading a book about stroke, I learned that injuries to the left hemisphere of the brain can indeed impact analytical thinking, as this hemisphere is typically associated with logical reasoning, and sequential analysis. I had found a scientific excuses for my stupid decision.

Insomnia affected my ability to sleep. It would open my eyes around 2 or 3 am in the morning. Then, I could not sleep anymore. My mind was restless and troubled. I was feeling disturbed and uneasy. In the morning, I was fatigued and easily irritated. Rather than experiencing a sense of renewal, I noticed that my mood had deteriorated further as compared to the state in which I retired to bed. My eyes reddened, mirroring the intensity of my emotions. They were like type IIB diamonds which glow when exposed to ultraviolet light. At work, exhaustion weighed heavily upon me, making it challenging to maintain focus and concentration.

There is a correlation between having trouble sleeping and feeling depressed. If one struggles to have restful nights, it can intensify their feeling of sadness. Inadequate sleep decreases one's ability to maintain a positive disposition and exacerbates negative thinking. Additionally, it has an impact on the functioning of our brains. When fatigue sets in, we experience a decrease in energy levels, a negative attitude, and are challenged to maintain focus and drive. A multitude of factors can exacerbate feelings of melancholy or despair. Establishing healthy sleeping routines and seeking support from qualified professionals can significantly enhance our overall well-being by ensuring sound sleep.

The irresistible appeal of depression was overwhelming. It appeared to be the only way out from the obstacles and hardships I was encountering. The assurance of relief from the enduring agony, be it physical or emotional, that were with me. Like Odysseus, I felt a strong desire to surrender to the sweet sorrow that depression promised.

My parents had been by my side since their arrival in Abu Dhabi. They have been and are one of my main sources of support. On one afternoon, much like many others, we were engaged in an online conversation. It had been about a month since their return to Italy when I had the courage to articulate my feelings to them.

In tears, I told them, "Mom, Dad, it is getting harder for me every day. I am struggling to stay positive and maintain my focus on recovery."

There was a momentary silence as my parents processed my words. Then, my mother reached out. With empathy, she said, "Sweetheart, we understand. We are here to support you." She paused, then added in a comforting tone, "Remember, since the first day after the stroke, you have shown incredible strength and determination. You cannot let these feelings consume you. There must be a way out."

I replied with determination, “You are right. I will not let these negative thoughts overpower me. I will do my best to regain my positivity and get back on track with my recovery.”

The next morning, my sister texted me. She was aware of my confession about my struggles. My parents had shared with her the conversation we had had the day before. She expressed her concerns about my mental and emotional health. She acknowledged the challenges I was facing. She reminded me that I had displayed strength and willpower to overcome any obstacle. I admitted that it was difficult for me to cope with the current circumstances. From that day, she texted me every day. She was checking in on how I was managing and holding up.

One morning, as I walked along the tranquil canal, the sun's golden rays dancing upon the water's surface, casting a warm glow, I found myself lost in introspection. My thoughts drifting towards the complexities of my own inner world. The weight of my emotions bore upon me. It was time to confront the truths I had been avoiding. And as I stood there, a realization began to take hold. It was a whisper at first. It grew louder and clearer with each passing second. "I am feeling down and discouraged. I have too many regrets!!” I finally said it aloud. The words hung in the air, a mix of vulnerability and relief.

Figure 32- Contemplative Strolls Along the Canal: Moments of Reflection.

I gazed into the rhythmic flow of the water. Albert Camus echoed in my mind: "Should I kill myself or have a coffee?" It was a disturbing question. Deep down, I knew that acting was imperative before it was too late. The words of my loved ones resurfaced. Their genuine concern blending with the existential ponderings of Camus. My parents, my sister, and Lei had all expressed their worries. At first, I resisted. I pretended that everything was fine. I had been trying to avoid accepting it. I was tangled in a web of cognitive dissonance, between acknowledging my struggle and pretending everything was fine.

Amid my inner dialogue, I recognized the significance of Camus' words. It was an invitation to choose life. To seek comfort in the simple pleasures that still awaited me. I could not allow myself to succumb to depression after all I had done since the stroke. I could not surrender to the weight of my emotions.

"I must have a coffee," I whispered to myself. A quiet declaration of defiance against the grip of depression. I acknowledged the darkness within me, but I also embraced the glimmer of hope that still burned. It was a fragile flame, extinguished, but worth fighting for. I was no longer in denial. So, I took a deep breath and told myself once more, “I am feeling down and discouraged. I am too negative and full of regrets and worries about my future. I am going to have a meltdown. I cannot continue like this!! I need to change my life. I need to fight and start afresh!!" This time was different. I was honest. It was my first step towards reclaiming my life and my sense of self.

I knew that I could not face this battle alone—I needed the support of my loved ones, the guidance of professionals, and the resilience within myself.

The canal, with its tranquil waters, seemed to mutter words of encouragement as I walked away. I carried within me the spirit of Camus' question, transformed into a resounding affirmation of life. I would have my coffee, savoring each sip as a reminder that amidst the darkness, there was still light to be found.

With each step, I felt a mix of apprehension and determination. I could not ignore the signs any longer. My thoughts turned to the Greek myth of Sisyphus. Forever rolling a stone up a mountain. Only to watch it tumble back down. I realized that I had been carrying my own burdens. My own metaphorical stone. It was time to acknowledge the weight it had placed upon me. I made a promise to myself: I would no longer suffer in silence. I would reach out to my loved ones. The support who had always been there for me. They had noticed my struggles and had offered their concerns and comfort. It was time to open myself to them, to share the depths of my emotions and the battles I faced within.

And beyond the support of my loved ones, I knew that seeking professional help was vital. Trained professionals could offer guidance, tools, and therapies to navigate this challenging journey.

In the next section, I will share the transformative moments and pivotal experiences that shaped my path to recovery.

In addition to my parents, Lei and my sister played an essential role in my recovery. However, approaching them about my personal discomfort was a different challenge altogether. I worried that they would not comprehend the intricacies of my struggles or the emotional burden I carried.

Dear Me,

I know you are afraid, but you can handle this.

Love,
Marco

Embracing the Light during Darkness

"Failing allows you to assess the situation, then pivot your approach, and move forward," was the advice given to me by one of the former CEOs of Etihad Airways. It has remained imprinted in my mind ever since. It was business advice, yet, I have applied it to my life after the stroke.

In this section, I invite you to witness my journey of triumph as I emerged stronger from the depths of personal crisis. Like a phoenix, I rose from the ashes of worry, anxiety, regrets, and negativity. Life can sometimes knock us down, leaving us broken and lost, and there is where I found myself. Stuck in my own personal crisis. Or like J.K. Rowling said, "Rock bottom became the solid foundation on which I rebuilt my life."

Just like the legendary Greek god Dionysus, I have experienced moments of starting anew and finding strength within me. Dionysus represents the idea of change and new beginnings, just like I have faced my own challenges and grown stronger. I appreciate the joy and happiness in life. I believed in the power of change and the many possibilities it brings.

When I reached the bottom of my despair, I discovered an inner strength I never knew existed. Besides my effort, the support and love of my cherished ones (family and friends) had an influence. They were there for me when I needed it.

"My attitude has always been, if you fall flat on your face, at least you are moving forward. All you must do is get back up and try again." - Richard Branson

Triumphing Over Personal Crisis after a Stroke

On March 20th, 2023, I woke early to stiffness in my right arm. It was earlier than the alarm. The pickup for work was at 8 am. I tried to reach for my watch to check the time, but my right hand did not move. I tried again, and it was still stuck. Every morning, I checked if the dream of my right-hand moving had manifested into a reality. I cursed under my breath and used my left hand to check the time. It was 5:12 am. I sat on the bedside and took a deep breath. Now I understand the essence of 'rock and roll.' It was my morning ritual to rise from the bed. First, I would rock back and forth, slowly transitioning to a sitting position. Then, with a swift roll, I would make my way to the bedside. Although not the most proper way to get out of bed, the rock and roll technique proved to be a speedy alternative. Another short night. The spastic snake coiled around my arm, constricting my muscles. My clenched fist desiring for a break. Seeking relaxation. I swung my legs over the edge of the bed, my feet touching the floor as I rose. With each step, my gait took on a limping style. I moved towards the bathroom, overcoming the obstacles in my path.

I splashed chilly water on my face and tried to wake myself up. I went to the kitchen and prepared a coffee. The caffeine kicks in the morning. Thousands of thoughts swirled in my mind. Were they dancing or engaged in a fierce battle? Heavy loads onto my heart and mind like Atlas condemned by Zeus to hold up the celestial spheres or the heavens on his shoulders for eternity. After my morning exercises, I went to work. Like almost every day for the last few months, I opened my journal and wrote the following letter to myself. I opened my heart. I could not continue like that anymore.

Dear Marco,

Negative thoughts come to us all. But when you speak to them aloud, you give them life. That is when they become a reality. Your dark reality.

It is time to decide, to take charge and move forward. It will not happen on its own. Arise and affirm, "It will not defeat me. No matter how hard it gets. No matter how disappointed and down I feel. I am going to win. I am moving on with my life."

It is a call to action against stress and negativity. Leave behind the burden of anxiety. Embrace a fresh start, a new chapter where you reclaim your happiness and inner peace.

Life seems to become just a repeat of the same old routine and getting out of bed to start your day feels like a chore, when what you are doing does not really matter.

The stroke took from you lots of things. Part of your identity. However, it was not solely its fault. You allowed yourself to distance yourself from your past life. It is time to reclaim what you loved and rebuild the connections that brought you happiness and fulfillment. Redefine your path and rediscover the joys that once filled your days.

You have the love and support of many people. You are strong. You can overcome this difficult moment. Believe in yourself and take that first step towards a brighter future. Remember, it is your life, and you have the power to shape it. Changes start from you. No one can change your life, only you.

Your future self will thank you once he knows that you did your best to make his present happy.

With determination and resilience,

Marco

I had no excuses. I had failed in my emotional and psychological recovery. I had let anxiety, worries and regrets fill my mind and soul. I felt like a stubborn pizza dough, resisting the chef's gentle kneading, refusing to rise. I sagged, deflated and devoid of the usual zest. I did not want to let down all the people who were there for me. It was the starting gun of my new race. I had to race myself. I sprinted towards a fresh start, ready to embrace the challenges ahead. It was not an overnight process, but a gradual transformation. Each day, I took steps forward. This journey is still ongoing. I am determined to make the most of it. To grow stronger every step of the way. Along my path, I encountered not only victories, but also setbacks and moments of worry. However, I persevered and stayed committed to the journey I had begun. Even when things got tough, I kept moving forward, determined to overcome any obstacles in my way.

"Stress is eating me alive. I feel anxious. Regrets are clouding my mind. I am scared about the future. I do not see the light at the end of the tunnel. What do I have to do to shake it off?" I expressed it to Lei that same evening. I shared my deepest emotions and shed tears in her presence. She urged me to adopt a positive mindset and embrace self-love. She suggested that I rediscover the power of faith. In the years we shared together, she had tried the same many times. Finding new joy in activities such as reading, writing, and recognizing the potential for future activities.

She told me, "Stop worrying about how everything is going to turn out. Put your trust in God. He will move the mountains and turn the tables in your favor. Everything is going to be fine, just believe it! Let go of yesterday. Let today be a new beginning and be the best that you can, and you will get to where God wants you to be!!"

I reached out to my sister, discussing the challenges I faced after the stroke. Her empathetic ear provided me with comfort and a sense of connection during this difficult time. She reminded me of her words when I was in the ICU, "My main worry was about your brain. Now we know it works. So, use it. The rest will follow. Nothing is impossible if you want it."

With Masoud, I explored potential adjustments to my work situation. His suggestions and insights provided me with valuable perspectives. We looked at how to adapt my work and duties to my post-stroke circumstances. He reminded me I was a senior manager. I was supposed to lead the team and provide guidance; I should not do engineers' duties anymore. I had to shorten my emails—no more lengthy and complex emails—to cope with my left hand only status. I had to delegate work and entrust the team with all my projects. My role was to provide my team with the necessary resources to implement the projects and take decisions when required.

Etihad Medical gave me the possibility to reduce my daily working hours by two hours. But I decided to work full time. I preferred to be at work than at home doing nothing. At work, my mind was busy. Less time and opportunities to worry about my present and future. With renewed drive, I got back to coding. I started a few new projects to help my team. I tried to learn new fields and applications. I was valuable again. My team never failed to support me. They were helping me. They accepted my limitations. A warm feeling spread through me every time my teammates called me Chief and Boss. It brought a smile to my face and filled me with a sense of happiness and gratitude. Their nicknames made me feel valued and respected, like an important leader on our team. They acknowledged my presence and relied on my guidance. It gave me a boost of confidence and reminded me of the strong bond we shared. They did everything to involve me and reduce any possible source of stress for me. I changed the way I approached work until then. No more 12 hours per day. No more work during weekends. My physical and mental health were coming first. They were the most important factors of my life equation.

I rejoined my running team and resumed the activity of walking. Both Saturday at Birdcage at Al Wathba and Sunday at Yas Island. As I walked at Birdcage, a feeling of happiness filled me up. Climbing up the hills, my calves started to ache. They had done the same many times in the previous two years. Going down, I was careful. I feared falling. I remembered what Metha had said. Going up was easier because gravity helped me. But going down meant fighting against gravity. In that moment, I felt a mix of excitement and nervousness. Each step I took was a victory over my fears and a sign of my determination. The pain in my calves and the fear of falling reminded me of the challenges I had overcome and how strong I had become. Walking at Birdcage with my running team meant more than exercising. It showed me that I could face any challenge and become stronger. Each step I took was a chance to prove to myself that I could do anything if I believed in myself.

I recognized the importance of ongoing psychological support and continued my sessions with a psychologist. These sessions provided a safe space for me to process my emotions, gain insights, and further develop coping strategies. Therapy focuses on understanding the "Why" behind our thoughts, feelings, and behaviors. It helped me heal from past hurts and learn better ways to cope with life.

I reignited my love for reading and learning, immersing myself in books and knowledge. Continuous learning catalyzes personal and professional growth. It keeps us adaptable, innovative, and open to new ideas. I went back to old loves like Stoicism, Greek Mythology and Classics, and social studies. I added a few new entries like stroke survivors' books and self-development. I studied the life and teaching of Napoleon Hill on positive mind. Lei introduced me to its famous quote, "Whatever the mind can conceive and believe, it can achieve," early on in my rehabilitation. With my colleague and friend, Nazaif, we adventured in looking for new business opportunities. From developing software applications to designing new products for one hand people like me. While there are similar products on the market, they are quite expensive and not easy to find. At the time of writing these words, we are still in the studying phase of our project.

In the end, “Everything is figureoutable,” like Marie Forleo wrote in her bestseller. Reading her book served as a reminder that, regardless of the challenges I was facing, I possessed the inner strength and capabilities to overcome any obstacle and transform into the person I was destined to become.

I listened to podcasts about stroke and self-growth. Here are a few: “The Mindset Mentor” by Rob Dial; “The Daily Stoic” by Ryan Holiday; “Recovery After Stroke” by Bill Gasiamis; “The School of Greatness” by Lewis Howes; and “The Mindvalley Show” by Vishen Lakhiani. They are forms of personal coaching. They focus on the "How" of achieving goals and making positive changes in our lives.

Furthermore, I went back to learning. I took some basic courses on Artificial Intelligence and its applications. I expanded my knowledge about coding and looked for new areas to learn. I followed courses in writing, especially memoir, and learned about book publishing and marketing. I continued personal growth.

I broke down my thoughts and issues into small chunks. I learned at work to break any problem into six chunks. It is deep enough to get to that bite-sized chunk. I could dissect them and tackle them one by one. Small problems are easier to tackle. I could focus on each individual aspect and find effective solutions. This method allowed me to address the challenges more efficiently and make progress towards resolving them.

I shifted my perspective on life, embraced the power of positive thinking, transformed my thinking, and elevated my mood. As I embarked on this journey of rising from the ashes, each of these pivotal moments laid the foundation for my triumphant transformation. They were the catalysts that propelled me forward, instilling hope, resilience, and a renewed sense of purpose in my life after a stroke.

Figure 33- Marco Walking at Birdcage with Kevin

Renovating My Thinking and Mood

Our mindset plays a significant role in the recovery process. After my meltdown, I adopted a positive outlook and I let go of frustrations and regrets. The stroke was not driving my life anymore. I took back the driver's seat.

"Isn't it nice to think that tomorrow is a new day with no mistakes in it yet?" This quote by L.M. Montgomery captures the essence of hope and the potential for a fresh start each day. Optimism and positive thinking have power in our lives. An optimistic mindset can have a profound impact on our well-being.

It is not about denying or ignoring life's challenges or difficulties. Instead, they involve cultivating a new mindset, finding the silver lining, and seeking solutions and positive outcomes.

The stroke was not my fault. But I took full responsibility for my recovery and for embracing the new life I was given. It would be different but still meaningful and fulfilling. It was up to me to act upon it. I rebooted myself. I changed my Operating System.

I underwent personal growth and transformed my thinking and mood. I learned to navigate the post-stroke phase with resilience and positivity. I selected a fresh start. I reprogrammed myself to find joy in new experiences. To seek the positive aspects of my post-stroke life. It was completely new for me. I was never optimistic before the stroke. Then I became a pragmatic optimist. I learned to approach life with a positive mindset while also being practical and realistic. It is a mindset that combines optimism, which is the belief that things will generally work out for the best, with pragmatism, which involves being practical and grounded in your approach to achieving goals.

Regret is a negative emotion that hinges on counterfactual thinking, Dr. Roese explains. It means producing fictional scenarios to convince ourselves that things could be better. "There are people who say, 'I live my life with no regrets,' but if we unpack it a little bit, I think we will recognize that pretty much everybody has [them]," Neal Roese, Ph.D., a social psychologist tells SELF. The lack of forgiveness is emotionally and physically damaging. I forgave myself. I let go of the regrets that I could have done something to prevent the stroke. I studied the concepts of fighting negativity, letting go, and acceptance. Zen Master Thich Nhat Hanh teaches that mindfulness, anger, sadness, and regrets can be doorways to peace and beauty. When we perceive things clearly, negative feelings cannot get hold of us.

I started journaling my emotions and thoughts. It was grief journaling. Writing them allowed me to bring some skepticism and context to my personal story. Experts recommend this practice for emotional regulation, managing anxiety, mindfulness, practicing self-care, and increasing self-awareness. Like fear, the past and the future are products of our mind. No amount of guilt can change the past, and no amount of anxiety can change the future. I could not change the past, but I could change my present and influence the future. Thoughts are shades through which the world we see can look altered. That is because we are prone to "cognitive distortions." Seeing our emotions written out might seem dramatic, but if we have had these types of thoughts before, we know how real they feel in the moment.

My mind was wandering all the time, either reviewing the past or planning. Through practicing mindfulness, I noticed when my mind wandered off. Mindfulness is a type of meditation. You focus on being aware of what you are sensing and feeling in the moment without interpretation or judgment. I practiced walking meditation. I focused on the experience of walking. I was aware of the sensations of standing and the subtle movements that kept my balance. I adopted breathing methods. I practiced guided imagery, and to relax the body and mind.

I embraced self-acceptance. It made me more confident in myself. I accepted every aspect of myself without exception. I learned to accept the parts of myself that I considered negative or undesirable. I acknowledged that my right hand was not moving. I accepted it may never work again. My right straight finger resembled E.T.'s finger. A touch of magic in my own uniqueness. I made fun of my own appearance. I mocked myself for my unfit figure that resembled Bibendum, the Michelin Tyre Man. Or Koda, Brother Bear. I was alternating the names by the situation.

My left hand accepted the challenge and started working harder to fine tune her movements and skills. She got stronger and smarter. I played darts to improve its coordination and control.

I stopped comparing myself to others and to whom I was before the stroke. I stopped complaining about everything I lost. They were important aspects of my life, but I had a new life to live. All the little things in life that I had instead. I was lucky to be alive. I had minor disabilities. I have prayed every day that they were only temporary. Otherwise, I was ok. No issues with my cognitive functions. My brain was working. No software glitches. Self-acceptance helped me control my emotions. It helped me to forgive myself. According to Dr. Srini Pillay of Harvard Medical School, acceptance and forgiveness go together. It led to self-compassion. As per researcher Kristin Neff, self-compassion is more worthy for our mental and emotional health than self-esteem. Self-compassion is giving yourself, "the same kindness and care you would give to a good friend." It made me kinder to myself when I failed and made me more resilient to setbacks, especially when my attempts to jog kept failing, one after the other. It helped me to be more authentic without worrying about others' judgments. I was free to be my whole self.

> **Because one believes in oneself, one doesn't try to convince others. Because one is content with oneself, one doesn't need others' approval. Because one accepts oneself, the whole world accepts him or her.**
>
> **- Lao Tzu**

I thought, if I believe in myself, I will not feel the urge to convince others of my worth. Being content with who I am, I will not seek external approval. By embracing myself wholly, the world will accept and acknowledge me for who I am. It is a liberating journey of self-belief and self-acceptance that shapes how I interact with others and how the world perceives me.

I set sharp, clear, and defined (SMART) goals. They made me accountable. I could measure them. Setting goals gave me a long-term vision and short-term motivation. You cannot do what you do not quantify. You cannot get better upon something that you do not control.

I took pride in the achievement of those goals. Every week, I extended my walking distance. I reached 8.5km in one day.

I celebrated even the smallest achievements during my recovery process. I adopted the theory of marginal gains (or, as it sometimes called, “microexcellence”). Sir Dave Brailsford revolutionized sport by introducing this theory. If you make a 1% improvement in a host of tiny areas, the cumulative benefits would be extraordinary. This approach changed the British cycling team from a mediocre performer to sixteen gold medals over two Olympics and seven Tour de France wins in eight years. I cultivated gratitude for each bit of progress, no matter how small. I found motivation in each step forward. Every walk and stair climbed. Any additional movement on my shoulder and arm. I was a young bird, timidly opening its wings for the very first time.

Every small victory was a significant contribution to my transformation over time. I improved my walking style. My knee got back in line, almost straight. No more excessive external swing, except when I had tired leg. My arm got a more relaxed stance. It lost its bent form. Spasticity reduced its tight grip on my muscles.

I adopted a growth mindset. Challenges were opportunities for personal growth and learning. You are only surrounded by challenges if you consider them a challenge.

From the Latin proverb, "Mater artium necessitas," which translates to English as, "Necessity is the mother of invention," my limitations and abilities were the driving factors. I produced new techniques for showering and dressing. I created my new cooking style. Stirring risotto was not an issue anymore. My strong right-hand grip was perfect for opening bottles and toothpaste. It was like a crocodile grasp. After several attempts, I perfected my one-hand pizza dough and fresh pasta processes.

Figure 34- Crafting delicate Italian Fettuccine: A Triumph of One-Handed Skill.

I understood that setbacks were part of the journey. I used them as lessons to continue my development. I refined the technique JD taught me months earlier to get in and out of the car. No more hitting the car frame with my right leg when getting out. I changed the sequence to counteract my limited knee and leg extension.

Life is suffering. It is one of the noble truth that Buddha taught. My life did not change 180 degrees in one moment. Life is not always easy or fair. It is filled with moments of suffering and hardship. I experienced sadness, pain, and disappointment along the way.

Every now and then, an internal voice would remind me of my disability and the possibility that it might be permanent. But I always tried to silence that voice and instead believe that God has a purpose for me. I held onto the hope that He would give me what was meant for me. That thought gave me strength to keep pushing forward.

The stroke decided to stay. My clenched hand and curled toes remind me every day. My curled toes made standing quite an adventure. I could feel the tightness of my leg arm muscles up to my brain. Because my foot was pointing outward, I could not wear open shoes or flip-flops. I had to wear closed shoes to walk. Spasticity was a new lifelong companion. But they made me stronger. Every time I had a negative thought, I replaced it with a positive one. I spoke in present tense to myself. I acknowledged the negative thoughts. I did not try to make them disappear. I faced them. I resolved them as much as I could. I did not hide them under the rug. I did not bury my head in the sand.

I became aware of my chimp and its patterns. When I spotted it, I screamed, "Stop," aloud, and told it how to behave. You can divide our mind into three main parts: the human, the chimp, and the computer as per Professor Steve Peters, 2012. The human is our rational, logical, and analytical side. It makes informed decisions—critical thinking. It considers the effects of our actions. The chimp is our emotional and impulsive side. The computer is the storage and processing system of our mind. It stores memories, experiences, and learned behaviors.

To live happier and more successful lives, we need to manage our chimp. This paradox encourages us to develop strategies and techniques to tame our chimps. We want the human in charge.

I acknowledged that emotional healing takes time. I asked for help when needed. I regularly opened myself with my family, especially my sister, Lei, and the psychologist. After shifting perspectives, I experienced personal transformation and growth. I embraced new beginnings. Appreciated small victories. Changed my perspective on challenges and cultivating self-compassion. I found strength and resilience. With an open mind and a willingness to embrace change, it was possible to create a post-stroke life filled with hope and optimism.

Finding Morals in Stroke Recovery

The moral of a story is the lesson or message that the story is trying to teach us. It is an important idea or value that we can learn from the story. Morals help us understand what is right or wrong, how to behave, or what to believe. It is like a guide or a reminder of how we should act or think in certain situations. The moral of a story can be different for each story, and it is up to us to think about what the moral might be and how it applies to our own life.

Each person's stroke recovery has a moral of its own. But there are a few potential morals, or a combination of, that someone might draw from their journey of recovering from a stroke:

1. **Resilience and Strength:** Morale emphasizes the resilience and inner strength one discovers while facing the challenges and obstacles that come with stroke recovery.
2. **Appreciation for Life:** It highlights a newfound appreciation for life and the things that might have been taken for granted before the stroke, such as good health, relationships, and everyday activities.
3. **Adaptability and Perseverance:** The morale focusses on the importance of adapting to a new normal and persevering through the physical and emotional difficulties of stroke recovery.
4. **Support and Connection:** It emphasizes the significance of support from loved ones, healthcare

professionals, and support groups, highlighting the power of human connection during challenging times.

5. **Personal Growth and Priorities:** Morale underscores the opportunity for personal growth and a reassessment of priorities, leading to a greater focus on self-care, personal fulfillment, and pursuing meaningful goals.

It is important to note that each person's experience and interpretation of their stroke and recovery will be unique, so the morale they derive from it may differ.

My moral of experiencing a stroke is "Resilience and Strength." A rubber band stretches but returns to its original shape. Resilience helped me to face challenges. Learn from them. Come out stronger on the other side. I was sad, frustrated, and scared at times but I found inner strength to keep going and adapting to new situations. Resilience taught me the importance of embracing change; seeking alternative paths.

> **Life is very interesting... in the end, some of your greatest pains, become your greatest strengths.**
>
> **-Drew Barrymore**

In the end, I have come to realize that my stroke, once my greatest pain, has transformed into one of my greatest strengths. We can discover meaning and purpose in the face of adversity. Life's challenges can be catalysts for transformation. There are opportunities for growth and fulfillment within difficult circumstances.

"I grew like a bamboo tree," is often used as a metaphor to convey the idea of personal growth and resilience. Bamboo is known for its fast growth and remarkable strength, making it a powerful symbol in many cultures. Bamboo can withstand strong winds and even intense storms by flexing with force rather than resisting it. Just as a bamboo tree can grow rapidly and reach impressive heights, the metaphor suggests that human beings have the potential for continuous growth and improvement. It encourages us to be adaptable, flexible, and open to change as we navigate the challenges and opportunities that come our way.

Rediscovering Faith

"Lord Jesus, I repented my sins. Come into my heart. I will make you my Lord and Savior!!" This is the end passage of each Joel Osteen's video. Joel Osteen and his wife are the pastors of the largest church in the United States, Lakewood Church in Houston, Texas. Osteen teaches a message of "hope, healing, and forgiveness." Its teaching is rooted in Pentecostalism. Physical healing and wellness were provided in Christ's atonement: "Jesus came that we might have a more abundant life. He came to carry our weaknesses, our sickness, our pain, so that we can walk in total freedom, peace, power, and purpose."

For Joel, success is a sign of God's favor and blessings. Having faith and positive thinking can attract prosperity and abundance into our lives. By many, he is seen more as an inspirational life-coach, instead of a herald of the gospel. But I did not mind his preaching about how people can improve their lives, be prosperous, and experience happiness. I could not see any fault in that logic. Can you?

I was born in Italy, a country with Catholic traditions. I grew up in Castel Gandolfo, a village on the outskirts of Rome. For centuries, it had served as the summer retreat for popes. During my early years, I attended a Catholic school for kindergarten and primary education. However, as I entered my teenage years, my fascination with books and politics overshadowed the Catholicism that had shaped my childhood.

Two of the authors who influenced my political thinking

were Karl Marx and Max Weber. Their writings and theories impacted how I viewed society and its structures. Marx's *The Communist Manifesto* introduced me to critical analyses of capitalism and its effects on individuals and society. One of Marx's most famous statements about religion is "Religion is the opium of the people." Marx believed that religion was a soothing balm that numbed the pain of exploitation and inequality experienced by the working class. He argued that religion enabled an unjust system by suggesting false hope and possibilities of a better life. Besides, Max Weber believed religion was a force for social change. Weber argued that Protestantism played a crucial role in shaping the values and behaviors of the people. According to Weber, Protestantism emphasized hard work, discipline, thrift, and the pursuit of individual success. Thus, it created a cultural and religious framework that encouraged the accumulation of wealth. It fostered capitalism. Weber also explored the concept of "disenchantment" in modern societies. Traditional religious beliefs and practices lost their significance and influence. He observed a shift towards rationalization in various aspects of life, including religion.

Before my stroke, I held an agnostic stance. I believed the existence of God or ultimate truth was unknown or unknowable. I neither affirmed nor denied the existence of a higher power. I recognized the limitations of human knowledge and chose to embrace a position of questioning and exploration rather than subscribing to any religious belief or completely denying it.

Early 20th-century interest in religion and mental health was sparked by Freud's view of religion as intrinsically neurotic. Freud described religion and its rituals as a collective neurosis.

In recent years, researchers have significantly increased their focus on the relationship between spirituality and health. Spirituality and religiousness (S/R) have been linked related to both physical and mental health. Most of the evidence on the relationship between S/R and mental health is positive. They show an inverse correlation between S/R and depression, suicide rate, substance use, and psychotic disorder.

Reba Riley, author of *Post-Traumatic Church Syndrome,* wrote, "Sometimes we must get lost to get found. Post-Traumatic Church Syndrome may be my story of physical and spiritual change, but it is also the story of everyone who has witnessed the way God can transform brokenness into beauty."

I was tired. I was lost in the maze of my thinking. There was no apparent exit to that maze. Everything was in a loop. I was drowning in the quicksand of negativity. "Paging the mother of lost boy wearing regrets, anxiety and stress, please proceed to customer service!!" I was looking for some help to change my thinking and beliefs about myself and what was around me.

Lei helped me reconnect with my childhood faith. She encouraged me to rediscover the faith that I had lost. She reminded me that I was still a beloved child of God, even more during my struggles. She encouraged me to pray. I tried it in the early morning. When everyone else was still asleep, I found solace in those quiet moments. I prayed in silence. I poured out my thoughts and I found comfort in a higher power. I prayed for my health, for my hand to move and heal. To run once more, with strength. To bring me happiness and wealth. To have the strength and inspiration to complete this book.

It was during those moments that I felt a sense of peace and renewed strength to face the challenges ahead. With Lei, I started watching Joel Osteen's videos. His videos and teachings have been part of my daily morning routine. His words were powerful and helped change the way I thought about things. His messages inspired me and gave me hope during tough times. The travel to get to the other side made me stronger and resilient. It reframed my thinking. I started to see the world in a different way, focusing on the good things. I learned to be grateful and appreciate the small joys that came my way. Life was good and had something amazing in store for me. I started believing in myself and moving forward, no matter what. Faith brought me comfort and strength. I forgave my past. Accepted my mistakes. Accepted who I was. Dropped my regrets. I stopped looking backwards. There was something better waiting for me. I opened my heart to a brighter future. I changed my mindset. I was new; different from the Marco of a month earlier. After 47 years, I was finally true to myself. It took time.

Similarly, to Dante entering the Empyrean—the place of pure light where God resides—I had to understand that God's love is at the center of the universe, setting everything else into motion.

> WHEN YOU FOCUS ON BEING A BLESSING, GOD MAKES SURE THAT YOU ARE ALWAYS BLESSED IN ABUNDANCE
>
> - JOEL OSTEEN

This quote deeply resonates with my reflections on life's journey. I have come to understand that shifting my focus from merely seeking blessings for myself to being a source of blessings for others, a beautiful transformation occurs. By embracing a mindset of kindness, compassion, and selflessness, I have experienced the profound impact of giving back to those around me. Whether through a helping hand, a listening ear, or a simple act of kindness, being a blessing to others has brought me a sense of fulfillment and purpose like no other. And in this journey of giving, I have witnessed the divine synchronicity that unfolds – the universe responding in kind with an abundance of blessings showered upon me. It is a profound reminder that true fulfillment lies in being a conduit of positivity and love, and in this reciprocity, I find joy and richness beyond measure.

Is it morally wrong to desire and pursue a happy and prosperous life? (This is a good title for another book.) I do not think so. I leave it up to everyone to decide on their own.

Some may argue that pursuing happiness and prosperity in a responsible and ethical manner is a natural and legitimate human aspiration. Many people aspire to have a fulfilling and prosperous life that includes both material abundance and a sense of well-being and contentment. The pursuit of happiness and the pursuit of prosperity are not necessarily mutually exclusive. I do believe that both can positively impact oneself and others, leading to a more fulfilling and meaningful life. On the other hand, some might caution against excessive attachment to material wealth and the potential negative consequences it can bring. They may emphasize the importance of spiritual growth, inner contentment, and the well-being of all beings over personal gain. According to Buddhist teachings, true happiness and liberation come from letting go of attachments, desires, and cravings. It encourages individuals to find happiness in simplicity, contentment in the present moment, and compassion for all beings.

Why not seek all of them in a balanced manner? It is okay to want both happiness and prosperity in life. Many people dream of having a good and successful life with lots of money and feeling happy inside. Wanting to be happy and successful is not a problem.

But it is also important to remember balance. We should not only care about money and stuff and forget about other important things like our friends, learning new things, and being kind to others. It is about finding a good mix of doing well financially and feeling good inside.

One ancient Chinese story that touches upon the subject of happiness and prosperity is the story of the fisherman and the businessman. There was a fisherman who lived by the sea. He was happy with his simple life of fishing, spending time with his family, and enjoying the beauty of nature. One day, a rich businessman visited him. He questioned why the fisherman did not work harder to catch more fish and become wealthy. The fisherman thought about it and decided to stick to his peaceful life. He realized that true happiness and prosperity did not come from having lots of money or possessions. Instead, it came from appreciating the things that truly mattered, like spending time with loved ones and enjoying the beauty of the world around him.

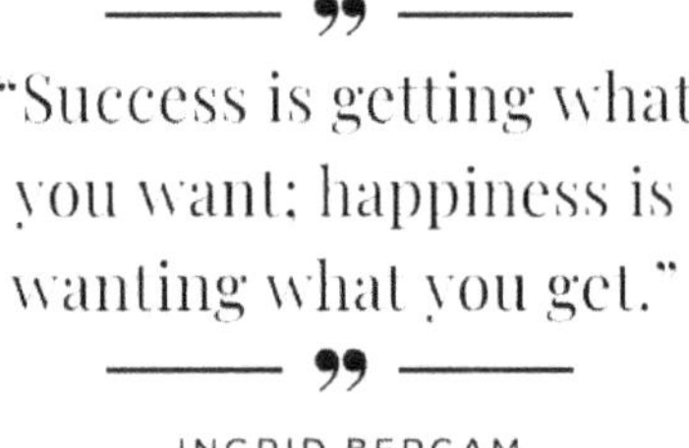

What is more valuable to you, happiness, or success?

Happiness has intrinsic value. While success and money, on the other hand, have extrinsic value. Happiness is an objective that many people aspire to. Most people also have a strong desire to be successful and prosperous in life. They believe that through this success, they will automatically become happier. Money cannot buy happiness, but it can provide access to the things we value in life, such as free time and peace of mind. According to psychologist Daniel Gilbert (2010), "Happiness is the goal of virtually all the decisions we make in life." We make decisions, considering if that decision brings us pleasure, a sense of wellbeing, happiness, or contentment.

Social studies have shown that poor people with access to regular cash flow developed a much higher sense of satisfaction about their health and life. Other studies and surveys hint that money may help buy happiness when used to meet basic needs. However, once basic needs are met, the happiness a person can gain from money may grow stagnant.

Besides, while happiness is a feeling correlated to better health and well-being, the obsession of being happy can be a formula for dissatisfaction. There is some evidence that the maniac pursuit of happiness is linked with a greater risk of depression.

According to philosopher Immanuel Kant, it is preferable to prioritize moral actions over the pursuit of happiness. While this perspective is valuable, this is not a philosophical book. Thus, we can move on from this discussion.

Money is unlikely to buy happiness, but it may help you achieve happiness to an extent. Buying a private jet "was my all-time goal," millionaire Mark Cuban told Magazine Money in 2017. "Because the asset I value the most is time, and that bought me time."

Look for things that will help you feel fulfilled. And beyond that, you can find happiness through other nonfinancial means, like spending time with people you enjoy or thinking about the good things in your life. Choosing whether to focus more on happiness, prosperity, or both is something personal. Some people might think that being peaceful and content is more important than having lots of money, while others might find joy in reaching their financial goals. The important thing is to figure out what makes you happy and successful in a way that feels right for you.

I always believed that every religion has something good to learn from. I had discussions with my Muslim and Hindu friends about the importance of health and wealth. Both religions value good health. They are precious treasures that allow us to have fulfilling lives. We discussed the idea of balance and moderation, understanding that we must not desire wealth at the expense of our health. We agreed that taking care of ourselves and others is important. True wealth goes beyond material possessions, encompassing inner contentment and spiritual well-being. I highlighted that Catholics believe in the power of prayer. They entrust their health and material needs to God. They pray for physical healing, strength, and well-being. They seek God's guidance and grace in matters related to health and wealth. Catholics are also called to trust in God's providence. He will provide for their needs according to His wisdom and love. It was a meaningful conversation. It helped us appreciate the wisdom within our different faiths. Our conversation highlighted the shared values and teachings in Islam, Hinduism, and Catholicism regarding the battle between health and wealth, while also displaying the unique perspectives within each faith.

The Psychologist

In an instant, my life took an unexpected turn when a stroke shook the very foundation of my existence. I found myself grappling with physical limitations and a whirlwind of emotions. The road to recovery seemed daunting and I knew that seeking professional guidance was vital to regain control over my life. So, I started a transformative journey with psychologists. First, I had face-to-face sessions at ProVita. After I went home, I continued the same path, but this time online.

The first time I sat in front of my computer screen, I was nervous yet hopeful. I logged into an online platform to connect with a psychologist. The initial encounter brought a sense of relief. He greeted me with empathy and understanding. He created a safe space for me to express my fears, frustrations, and uncertainties.

A stroke is not merely a physical ailment; it takes a toll on one's emotional well-being as well. Through internet conversations, I unveiled the emotional turmoil that resided within me. I shared my fears of never fully recovering. My frustrations with the limitations I had. The sense of loss that enveloped me. The psychologists helped me confirm these emotions. He reassured me that it was normal to have such feelings after such a life-altering event.

We explored the aspects of my identity that remained intact. The strengths I possessed, and the new opportunities for growth that lay before me. These conversations helped me to reframe my perception and cultivate a new sense of resilience.

Grief and loss became my constant companions after the stroke. I mourned the life I once knew. The activities I could no longer engage in, and the relationships that were strained by the burden of my condition. I learned to navigate the stages of grief. I allowed myself to process the emotions associated with each phase. The internet conversations served as a lifeline. I shared my sorrows. I received guidance on how to honor my losses while embracing the possibilities that lay ahead.

The stroke had a ripple effect on my relationships, straining the bonds with my loved ones. The psychologists provided guidance on open communication and understanding within my support network. We discussed the ways to express my needs, set boundaries, and seek the support I required. I rebuilt my relationships, fostering a sense of connection and mutual support.

They gave me coping mechanisms to navigate the challenges I had to face. We explored stress management techniques. Mindfulness practices. Adaptive strategies to address the physical and emotional hurdles I encountered. These tools became invaluable as I faced setbacks. They allowed me to overcome obstacles and maintain a positive outlook on my recovery. He advised me to write down my emotions and experiences. I wrote about stroke's impact. I penned a letter to Gabriele. I showed my innermost self, feeling exposed and raw.

The psychologists helped me to reclaim my connection with my son. I gained insights into our relationship, fostering understanding and empathy. I embraced my role as a parent, with open communication and nurturing our bond. As our relationship blossomed, I witnessed the positive impact of our renewed connection on both of us. Our moments of shared laughter, heartfelt conversations, and mutual support became the building blocks of a strong and resilient bond that will undoubtedly stand the test of time. Throughout this period, I came to realize just how important Gabriele is to me and how incredibly proud I am of the young adult he has grown into.

The professional guidance after my stroke was transformative. I navigated the complex emotional landscape of recovery. I explored my identity. I developed coping mechanisms to face the challenges that lay before me. Psychologists were anchors in my journey. They guided me towards acceptance, resilience, and renewed hope. The power of virtual conversations transcended physical limitations. It allowed me to access the support I needed from the comfort of my own home. I am grateful for the role of professional guidance in rebuilding my life after the stroke.

Embracing the Unthinkable: A Life Transformed

My journey of self-discovery started in the desert. Today, 10 months have passed since that day, and it has been 18 months since the last time I went to the beach. Now, I find myself at the beach in Abu Dhabi, with the sand—of a different type from day one—touching my feet. The waves roar, and the water currents push and pull me, like a yoyo tugged back and forth. To maintain stability, I sink my feet into the soft and wet shore. The waves relentlessly try to knock me down with each passing surge. The foamy white crests drawing patterns on the shore, resembling Salvador Dali's surrealistic paintings. I can perceive hundreds of different shapes, each one with its own meaning. I stand there, taking it all in. Every step I take in the shallow water serves as a reminder of the power of the stroke. I need to be present, consciously lifting my right foot. The water, aided by the wet sands, tries to make me trip. At the beach, I feel more like a walrus or a polar bear than a person.

Marcus Aurelius wrote, "The art of living is more like wrestling than dancing." I write, "Sharing a life with a stroke can be even harder."

On September 8th, 2022, something bad happened. It is called a stroke. It caused me to get sick and feel emotional in its aftermath. It was like opening a Pandora box of troubles that I had to deal with. The stroke made my body feel weak and sick. I had to get medical help and work hard to get better.

But it also made me feel scared and unsure about things. It made me think about life and what really matters to me. It was a time when I had to look inside myself and face my fears and feelings. Even though the stroke brought a lot of challenges, it also helped me grow and learn about myself. I realized that I am strong and can manage difficult things. Opening this box of troubles was hard, but it taught me that it is important to take care of both my body and my emotions. It reminded me to ask for help when I need it. To face my feelings instead of ignoring them. It made me stronger and helped me appreciate the strength we all have inside us. I found support from people who cared about me. They helped me get through the tough times and feel better.

My relationship with Lei got stronger. She helped me to look at my life from a different perspective. She made me rediscover faith. She introduced me to new thinking. She made me believe in myself. I could achieve everything I wanted; I just had to put in the work and keep going on—every day, one step at a time. Rome was not built in one day. In my journey of recovery, I have embraced the art of patience wholeheartedly.

I have come to understand that healing takes time, and progress is not always immediate. Like a delicate flower blooming, my body and mind require nurturing and time to grow stronger. Before the stroke, I was incredibly impatient, always seeking immediate results. However, in the wake of this life-altering event, patience has emerged as my greatest ally, leading me through the highs and lows of the recovery process. I remind myself that "Patience is the key that unlocks the doors of life's greatest achievements," and I hold onto this wisdom with unwavering faith. Each day, I cultivate patience as a virtue, knowing that it is the foundation for reaching new heights and overcoming obstacles. Through this virtue, I find strength, hope, and a sense of peace, knowing that with time and perseverance, I will witness the blossoming of my recovery.

Believe it or not, patience is a virtue that can be cultivated and nurtured over time. Indeed, patience is a virtue that not everyone knows how to manage or cultivate. It requires conscious effort and a willingness to embrace the process of growth and learning. The stroke taught me that patience is "sacred," but it is also an art that we develop over time. Through the challenges and setbacks, I faced during my recovery, I came to understand that life itself can be a powerful teacher, imparting the strength needed to cultivate patience. Like an artist refining their craft, I learned to embrace the journey of patience, allowing it to shape me into a resilient and steadfast individual.

This stroke was a great opportunity to grow closer to my parents and sister. To close some old emotional wounds. In the past, we had some misunderstandings, and we went on for a few years without any contact. Reflecting on that, I realized that life is short. Memento mori, which means "remember that you must die" in Latin, is a reminder of our own mortality, our mistakes and failures, and the inevitable transformation of life into death. The Stoics used memento mori to set priorities and provide meaning. For me, it holds deep personal significance. It made me understand that I had lost time with my family—precious time, the only thing we cannot buy in this life. Time is priceless, as the famous credit card company advertised, “There are some things money can't buy; for everything else, there's Mastercard.”

My parents spent six months by my side. The three months I was at ProVita and the first three months at home. They returned to Italy in early March 2023. They left when I was ready to continue my journey independently with Lei. Their love, care, and dedication played an integral role in my recovery and transition to living alone.

In those six months we spent together we had so many laughs. They helped me with my recovery. They were with me at every rehabilitation session. They celebrated any victory and supported me when I faced setbacks. They were there with me. They provided a shoulder to lean on and an empathetic ear to listen. Their emotional support gave me the strength to face my health challenges head-on. They provided a safe space where I could express my fears, frustrations, and hopes. They helped me maintain a positive mindset throughout my recovery. We celebrated progress together. Since they left Abu Dhabi, they kept supporting me with encouragement, through daily talks via the Internet. They kept celebrating any improvement, even the smallest one. My father keeps ensuring I book all medical appointments and I have enough spare for my daily medications.

In my living room, I have a frame with photos capturing instances from my childhood—moments with my parents and sister. Every time I look at them, I am grateful to have them in my life. I took time to reflect on our relationships and found the courage to express my feelings to my family, saying, 'Vi voglio bene!!!' which means "I love you" in Italian. And I always will. This stroke helped me to get closer to my parents and sister, and I will not waste this opportunity.

I reconnected with my sister. We forged a bond stronger than ever before. I cherish one precious picture displayed in my living room. It captures a moment of pure joy from our childhood days at the beach. We immersed ourselves in the sandy shores, building intricate sandcastles while bravely battling the crashing waves that threatened to erode our creations.

Throughout the past months, my sister and I engaged in countless conversations. We discussed my journey and the challenges I faced post-stroke. My sister emphasized the importance of prioritizing my physical and mental well-being above all else. She repeatedly reminded me of how fortunate I was to have survived the stroke. She urged me to focus solely on the aspects of life that truly mattered.

My sister had and she still has a profound impact on my journey towards recovery. Her compassion and wisdom guided me towards renewed determination. She instilled hope and reminded me of the immeasurable value of love and family during times of adversity.

***

Writing this book was a cathartic experience. Aristotle created the word catharsis—from the Greek kathairein meaning "to cleanse or purge"—to describe the release of emotional tension audience experienced while viewing dramatic tragedy. Today, the word "catharsis" is used in reference to any experience of emotional release or cleansing brought about by a work of art.

It has been a journey through my life. It helped me let go of my emotions and find healing. I shared my memories and experiences on paper. It made me feel better. It was a safe way for me to express my thoughts and feelings. Writing my story helped me understand myself better and accept who I was and who I became afterwards. It was a way for me to discover my strengths and learn from my challenges. In the process, I found myself transformed in a positive way. By sharing my memoir, I wanted to connect with others who may have gone through similar things. Finishing my memoir was a big moment for me. It helped me find peace with my past and embrace who I am today. Writing my memoir was like therapy, and it helped me grow and become a stronger person. It was almost a mystical and spiritual exploration. In the process, I found myself transformed in a positive way. Writer André Aciman said that people write memoirs because they want to create another version of their lives. I have confidence my story brings hope. It shows that miracles can happen in tough places. Someone wrote to me, “Your story is important to share. I pray others will read your book, follow your videos and be open to your message.” Someone else said, “You only live once, but if you do it right, once is enough." And I had the luck to live twice. That morning I was rebirthed in my own body, I was wandering through, flowing on (Sa□sāra) from the old Marco to the new Marco.

In the aftermath of my stroke, I found myself confronted by a stark reality. Everything that had once defined me—the physical abilities, the autonomy—had been abruptly stripped away. The person I once was seemed lost, swallowed by the void of uncertainty. However, amidst the rubble of my former self, I discovered a remarkable opportunity for rebirth and reinvention. Indeed, the process of self-discovery was not without its trials and tribulations. There were days when doubt and frustration threatened to engulf me, when the weight of my limitations felt suffocating. I learned that being patient during frustrating times can transform life into play and make it feel less like work.

I am filled with gratitude for the miraculous transformation that unfolded in the wake of my stroke. The desert of despair and uncertainty, which initially seemed insurmountable, has become the backdrop against which my journey of self-discovery has unfolded. This final chapter marks a significant milestone—a testament to the power of the human spirit and the capacity for growth in even the most challenging circumstances.

I discovered appreciation for life's simplest joys—the warmth of the sun on my skin, the sound of laughter, the gentle touch of a loved one, good moments shared with friends.

I discovered that happiness need not be tethered to the external trappings of success, but rather derived from within, from a deep wellspring of gratitude and acceptance.

Discontentment can be dangerous. The key to finding contentment is accepting ourselves and what we have. By doing so, we can pave the way towards inner peace, where we feel truly at peace with ourselves and our circumstances. It is about appreciating the present moment and finding happiness in what we already possess. True contentment begins within, and it leads us on a path towards lasting peace and happiness.

Affirmations and self-talk hold incredible power. When we speak positive words to ourselves, we uplift our spirits, boost our confidence, and shape our mindset. Affirmations are the little pep talks that we give ourselves to cultivate self-belief and motivation. I always speak in present tense to myself. I keep repeating affirmations such as "I am a writer," “I am a runner," “I am a billionaire," "I am worthy," or "I can overcome challenges."

To further enhance its impact, I have incorporated stroke recovery and writing references into my work laptop password. Due to security requirements, I must change the laptop password every few months, and during each update, I alternate between these meaningful subjects. This practice not only reinforces the positive mantras but also keeps my mind engaged in the journey of recovery. Writing down those short affirmations multiple times a day solidifies their significance and acts as a continuous source of encouragement.

I am rewiring my thinking patterns to create a positive internal dialogue. Self-talk is the ongoing conversation we have with ourselves in our minds. By choosing to speak kindly, encouragingly, and compassionately to ourselves, we can nurture a healthy and empowering mindset. The power of affirmation and self-talk lies in their ability to shape our thoughts, emotions, and actions, ultimately leading us towards greater self-confidence, resilience, and personal growth.

"I find it difficult to depend on outside motivation. Your best bet is to find motivation inside you," I read this comment on one of the stroke survivors support groups. Relying on outside motivation can be tough, it changes and may not match our goals. Instead, the strongest source of motivation is within us. Internal motivation comes from our deepest desires, values, and dreams, driving us to reach our goals. When we use this inner motivation, we find purpose beyond external influences. Fueled by our own fire, we face obstacles with determination, stay committed in tough times, and keep pushing ahead. Embracing self-motivation not only empowers us to take charge of our lives but also fosters a profound sense of fulfillment as we witness our own growth and accomplishments. In the pursuit of our goals, looking inward can be the key to unlocking our full potential and realizing the extraordinary possibilities that lie within us.

Beside the teaching of Pastor Joel Osteen, I found pleasure and support on the words of Napoleon Hill. He is a renowned author and motivational speaker. He is considered the pioneer of the self-help genre. Through his timeless work, "Think and Grow Rich," Hill encapsulated a philosophy that continues to inspire generations. He emphasizes the power of positive thinking, perseverance, and the development of a success-oriented mindset.

Few of his quotes left a mark on me:

"Whatever the mind can conceive and believe, it can achieve." This quote encapsulates Napoleon Hill's core belief in the power of positive thinking and the influence of our thoughts on our potential for success.

"The starting point of all achievement is desire." Hill emphasizes that a burning desire is the driving force behind accomplishment. It is the foundation upon which all achievements are built.

"Strength and growth come only through continuous effort and struggle." Hill recognized that growth and personal development occur when we push ourselves beyond our comfort zones and persevere through adversity.

"Don't wait. The time will never be just right." Hill encourages individuals to act and seize opportunities without delay, emphasizing the importance of overcoming procrastination.

"Set your mind on a definite goal and observe how quickly the world stands aside to let you pass." This quote highlights the power of clarity and focus, suggesting that when we set our minds on specific goals, the universe aligns to support our endeavors.

I continue to dream big. My dream to compete and complete a 100km mountain race is still intact. The thought of crossing that finish line fills me with determination and excitement. Every day, I dedicate time and effort to training and strengthening my legs. I work hard to make them stronger and better. I am a runner, and I will run a 100km race somewhere, sometime. I am still on track to reach one of my rehabilitation goals: To run again within two years! However, because it is not possible to move from zero to hero, I have set intermediate goals. More reasonable and achievable ones. The first step is to jog a few meters, then, slowly increase the distance until I transition from jogging to running. At that point, I will build strength and distance as well. These goals are achievable. I just need to put in the effort and do the work to reach them.

To loyally uphold my long-term aspirations, I have taken a significant step—registering for the upcoming ADNOC Abu Dhabi Marathon scheduled for mid-December 2023. I am thrilled to be part of the 10km session, where my intention is to walk and possibly jog if my strength allows; otherwise, I will walk with determination. In pursuit of my goals, I have embraced a daily regimen of exercises. I take to the outdoors for a walk whenever weather permits, or I hit the gym for sessions on the treadmill, complemented by workouts on the elliptical, leg press, and leg curl machines. My commitment extends to daily stair-climbing, whether in the comfort of my home or within the workplace. And for those moments when the gym does not attract me, I turn to my static bike at home or enjoy invigorating swims in the rooftop pool of my building. While training in preparation for the ADNOC 10km, I also took part in several charity walks in Abu Dhabi.

Figure 35- Marco after completing the "Walk for Inclusion" event in Abu Dhabi.

The words of JD, "practice makes perfect," echo in my ears. Little did I know that this quote was originally attributed to Bruce Lee. The full quote elaborates further, "After a long time of practicing, our work will become natural, skillful, swift, and steady."

During my training sessions, I encounter moments that feel like short-circuits in my mind. Doubts creep in, and I begin to question whether I will ever achieve a satisfactory level of recovery. When this happens, I must pull myself out of that mindset, enabling me to enter a more tranquil state. It is akin to a dog trainer managing a hyperactive dog. Additionally, I remind myself that I have made important progress since the day I left the hospital.

I aim to maintain a balanced length for each exercise session, considering my current limitations post-stroke. My endurance is not what it used to be, and I have encountered challenges with neurological fatigue, which tends to set in after about an hour of continuous exercise. To manage this, I occasionally spread my sessions with short rest breaks, allowing me to extend my overall workout duration while ensuring I do not push myself too hard.

Certainly, due to the neurological principle of muscle memory, I came to understand that my initial focus should be on retraining both my mind and body to regain movement, laying the foundation before incorporating strength training. I encountered this concept firsthand when I began cooking with my left hand. Once merely a supporting player to my dominant right hand, now it has taken charge of everything. It embarked on a journey, starting with mastering the basics before progressing to the more advanced levels of cooking. It is akin to how children learn the alphabet before moving on to constructing whole words and sentences in their writing.

Finding inspiration and encouragement from fellow stroke survivors in online support groups proved to be a turning point in my recovery journey. Their shared stories of resilience and triumph after two to five years post-stroke filled me with hope and determination. Holding onto these successful accounts, I envisioned my own path to reclaiming my love for running. While a 100km race might be a lofty goal, I realized that any distance completed by running would be a tremendous achievement.

When I first arrived at ProVita, Kevin and Jovi gave me a book titled *EPIC RUNS of the WORLD*. Every time I glance at it on my living room shelf, a surge of motivation washes over me, compelling me to train harder. I know they gave me the book as a source of inspiration, and its title brings back cherished memories of the adventures we once shared together—scaling steep hills and mountains in the UAE. The book's presence fuels my determination, and I am confident that one day, we will embark on such thrilling journeys again. I believe in the promise of running once more, hand in hand, embracing the joy of shared experiences.

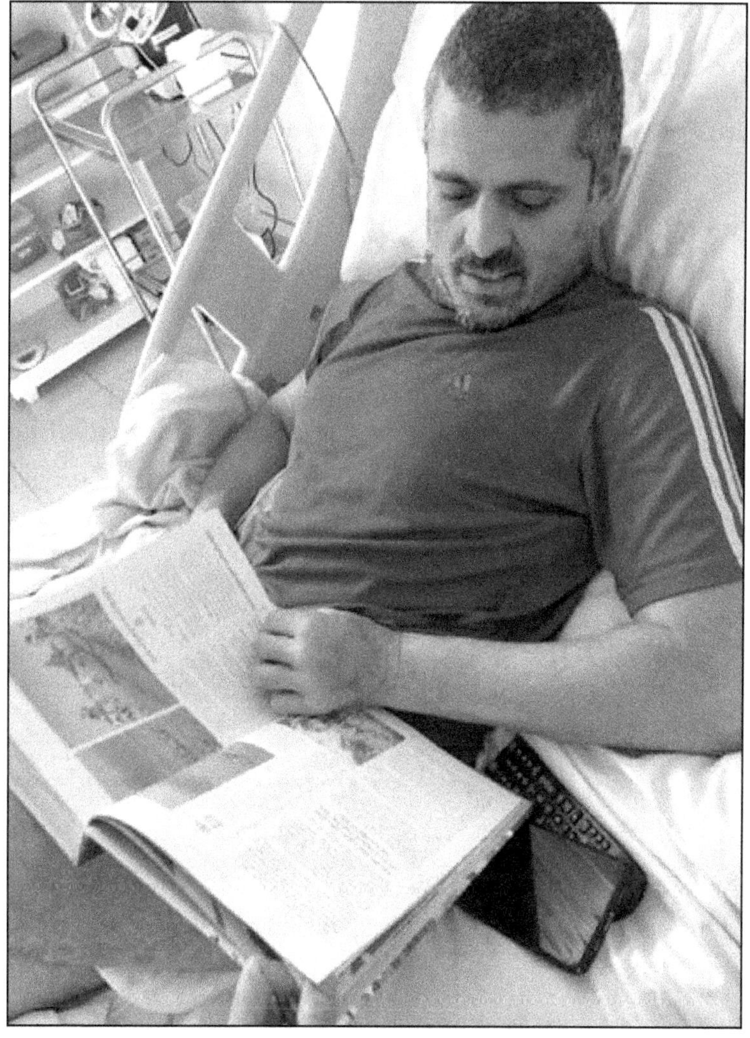

Figure 36- Marco turning the pages of "EPIC RUNS of the WORLD."

***

Every day, I pray for the puppeteer to mend the broken string and regain control of my leg and hand. The puppet inside me longs to use both hands and run freely once more. Every evening, I speak with my hand, asking her, "When are you coming back to me?" When I do that, Lei tells me, "She will come around on her time."

I always quote Dr Taylor, J.B. In her book, *My Stroke of Insight: A Brain Scientist's Personal Journey* (2009), she said that she took five long years to be able to jump from rock to rock without looking at where her feet were landing after her stroke. I know there is still hope for me.

I also aspire to be a successful writer, and I believe that the memoir I am currently working on has the potential to become a best-selling book. With each word I write, I envision my story touching the hearts of readers around the world.

I am filled with conviction that my journey of writing extends far beyond this current book. One of my future literary endeavors will undoubtedly be inspired by my first race, whenever and wherever it may take place. Should circumstances lead to an alternate path, I have a solid plan B in mind, ready to embark on an equally captivating writing adventure. Moreover, I find myself intrigued by the prospect of delving into research about spasticity and stroke recovery, recognizing the potential for multiple books in this area. The idea of weaving knowledge, personal experiences, and insights into these literary works excites me, and I am eager to share valuable information with others on similar journeys. As the pages of my future books unfold, each one will be a testament to my resilience and dedication to growth, not only in running but also in exploring new horizons through the power of writing.

These dreams fuel my motivation and drive me to keep pushing forward, no matter the obstacles I may face. I hold onto the belief that with dedication, perseverance, and a little bit of luck, I can turn these dreams into reality.

My journey of self-discovery continues. Every day. An ever-evolving narrative of embracing the unknown, celebrating small victories, and cultivating a belief in the limitless potential within. The desert, once a symbol of devastation, is now a testament to the strength of the human spirit, where miracles are born.

Everything is temporary, even life. Our lives can feel better by absorbing in the here and now. As we obtain the ability to be present, we will become happy.

Life, even after a stroke, is still beautiful. It reminds me of the powerful movie, *Life is Beautiful* by Roberto Benigni. Amidst the darkest of times, a father creates moments of joy and love for his family. Similarly, in the face of challenges, we can find beauty and hope. It is about cherishing simple pleasures, finding strength in our resilience, and embracing the precious moments that make life worth living. Despite the hardships, there is beauty in the connections we make, the strength we discover within ourselves, and the resilience that allows us to keep moving forward. Life, with all its ups and downs, is a beautiful journey waiting to be embraced.

Today, as I pen the final words of this memoir, I am humbled by the enormity of the transformation I have undergone. The stroke, once perceived as a cruel twist of fate, has become the catalyst for profound personal growth. I stand tall, not despite my limitations, but because of them. They have become the brushstrokes that paint the portrait of my resilience. I can say aloud that it is not a stroke defining who I am. I am the one deciding who I am and whom I want to be.

I discovered that using self-irony as a form of therapy can be helpful in relieving tension. One of the secrets to a happy life is not taking ourselves too seriously. By embracing self-irony, we can make life more enjoyable and fun. An example of this is Charlie Chaplin. He had a talent for turning his personal tragedies into comedic films that brought laughter to the world. Through his irreverent humor, he was able to exorcise his own personal dramas by blending elements of both drama and comedy. His ability to find humor in difficult situations allowed him to connect with audiences and bring joy to their lives.

When I am in the pool, I playfully imagine myself as a turtle beaten by a shark. The right fins have been cut. Embracing this lighthearted perspective adds a touch of humor to my swimming experience, reminding me to enjoy the journey and appreciate the uniqueness of each moment.

When Lei assists me with showering, my mind often drifts to images of elephants. I have witnessed these magnificent creatures being tenderly washed and scrubbed at various elephant sanctuaries in East Asia through television. Just as these elephants are cared for with gentle precision, Lei's support and care during my shower evoke a similar sense of compassion and attentiveness.

Similarly, Lei and I have our own comedy show. It is called "stroke o'clock!" It is the time for some hilarious mix-ups and funny mishaps. As I attempt to put on a t-shirt using my teeth to help my left hand or to put on socks like a contortionist. Or when I try to butter my toast. But hey, laughter is the best medicine, right? So, let us roll with it and turn stroke o'clock into a comedy hour full of giggles and grins. Who knows what hilarity awaits at the stroke of the hour! Embracing the humor in these moments lightens the load and reminds me to take life with a smile.

I am happy and content with myself and whom I became. I am pride of the reflection in the mirror. I reached inner peace. I tamed my inner demons. Or like Richard David Carson titled his book, *Taming Your Gremlin*. We can reach inner peace by tapping into a blissful state of mind in the middle of our hectic lives. I celebrate everything that comes into my life. Oprah Winfrey once said, "The more you celebrate your life, the more there is in life to celebrate." "Each day offers a reason to celebrate. Find it and experience true bliss!!" Amy Leigh Mercree encouraged.

A positive mindset is everything. The mindset is a powerful factor that influences our experiences and outcomes in life. It is said that 99% of our body is made up of empty space, highlighting the vastness and potential within us. Our thoughts and beliefs decide how we see the world.

By cultivating a positive and growth-oriented mindset, we

can unlock our full potential and overcome challenges. It is through our thoughts and mindset that we can manifest our goals and aspirations. Embracing a mindset of possibility and abundance allows us to tap into the limitless opportunities that surround us. Just as the empty space within our bodies holds immense potential, our minds have the power to shape our reality. With the power of our mindset, we can create the life we desire filled with growth and fulfillment. When faced with the life-altering effects of a stroke, one may feel that the road ahead is daunting and uncertain. But within this challenging landscape lies the unwavering capacity for growth and transformation, even in the face of adversity.

A stroke can be a turning point, disrupting the familiar rhythms of life and leaving us to grapple with the profound changes it brings. However, it is essential to remember that it is never too late to make positive changes in our lives, even after experiencing significant events like a stroke. With courage and determination, we can embark on a new chapter, focusing on becoming the best version of ourselves, one step at a time. It is never too late to make changes in our lives. We all have the capacity for growth and transformation, no matter our age or circumstances. It takes courage and effort to make changes, but the rewards are worth it. When we focus on becoming the best version of ourselves, we can live more fulfilling and meaningful lives.

Recovery from a stroke demands both physical and emotional effort. It requires perseverance to relearn skills that were once second nature and the strength to navigate the emotional toll it may take. It is a path that necessitates self-compassion, as progress may not always be linear, and setbacks may occur. But every small victory and each triumph over challenges becomes powerful affirmations of our inner strength and tenacity.

Throughout this journey, support from loved ones, healthcare professionals, and the stroke survivor community can be invaluable. Together, we create a network of encouragement and understanding, weaving a safety net of empathy and encouragement.

As Sinatra sang in 1945, "You'll never walk alone." Similarly, as stroke survivors, we shall never truly be alone. Though some of us may have experienced ostracization from friends or, in extreme cases, even family, we must remember that there exists a thriving community of survivors and fighters, always ready to offer help and support. They will never pass judgment on us; instead, they will embrace and accept us for who we are. In their understanding and compassion, we discover a network of individuals united by shared experiences, and together, we journey towards healing, strength, and hope. I personally found immense support, inspiration, and encouragement within these support groups. They provided a safe space where I could freely express myself, seek advice, ask questions, and feel fully accepted for who I am.

In the process of recovery, the stroke survivor must rediscover the essence of hope—the profound belief that a brighter future is possible, no matter how dims the present may seem. With every determined step and every small accomplishment, the darkness begins to recede, and the sunrise of renewal starts to bathe the soul in a gentle glow.

As the days unfold, the stroke survivor shall learn to embrace their newfound resilience, witnessing the profound transformation that emerges from within. The courage to face challenges head-on and the effort invested in every milestone become the foundations of growth.

Like Pink Floyd sings in their song, *Fearless*, "I'll climb the hill in my own way," the path to recovery is unique to everyone, shaped by personal experiences, aspirations, and strengths. It becomes a testament to the human spirit's boundless potential for renewal and adaptation.

And so, as the stroke survivor's journey continues, they become an inspiration not only to themselves but also to those around them. Their unwavering determination in the face of adversity touches the hearts of others, fostering a ripple effect of hope and encouragement.

We are reminded of the transformative power of the human spirit—a reminder that it is never too late to embark on a journey of growth, healing, and becoming the best version of ourselves.

I want to emphasize the significance of having a supportive and understanding environment. Without my loved ones, I might not have found the strength for my transformation. They served as catalysts, igniting the transformation within me and propelling me towards change. When people tell me,

"You are an inspiration!" I get emotional. I can feel their love and support. They fuel my engine to keep going forward. Every day.

It is hard, it is still so fuck@ing hard living every day with a stroke, but I have learned to adapt. I use my left hand for everything. I have found ways to manage spasticity. I live a full and productive life. I am grateful for that. Because of an old rehabilitation saying, "Use it or lose it," I am doing everything not to neglect my right side, especially my hand. I will use it as much as possible. To grab the milk bottle while I open it with my left side. To hold the coffee pods in the morning while I try to open the package. I even try to fit the scissors on my right hand, but the spasticity does not allow it—YET. When I cannot make use of my right hand, I would try to use any part of my body or any object to help me with my tasks. I am still an engineer and finding solutions to technical problems is part of my everyday duties at work.

Life with a stroke is like an annual pass at the amusement park. One day you are on a roller-coaster. The next day you relax and enjoy a lazy river. Unfortunately, I am not the one to decide which ride to take. There are millions of people living with stroke. It is possible to live a full and happy life. Do not give up. Like the famous American baseball player Babe Ruth said, "It is hard to beat a person who never give up."

Have you ever heard that the gut is our second brain? But what exactly does it mean? The gut plays a crucial role in supporting the brain and its functions. Through the intricate communication network known as the gut-brain axis, the gut and the brain interact and influence each other. The gut produces neurotransmitters, such as serotonin, which play a vital role in regulating mood and emotions. It also houses trillions of bacteria known as the gut microbiota, which produce various substances that impact brain health. Additionally, the gut engages in the production and regulation of certain hormones and immune responses that can affect brain function. Then, we need to take care of our gut for our stroke recovery. Like we do for our body. It is more do not than do in this case. Remove late-night snacks. Let us reduce caffeine and alcohol consumption. Let us cut on sugar and processed food. Instead, let us eat whole foods and fibers. Add healthy fats to our diet. Exercise and listen to our bodies.

***

Inspired by Maggie Whittum with her "The GREAT now what?" I ask the same question to myself, "Now what?" It prompts me to reflect on my goals, aspirations, and the direction I want to take. It challenges me to consider my values, passions, and the actions I need to pursue to fulfill my desires and contribute to my personal growth and the world around me. "Now what?" encourages me to embrace curiosity, seek new possibilities, and make choices that align with my authentic self. It prompts me to explore the depths of my existence and find meaningful paths forward. I am ready to keep working toward my recovery. To share my experience and encourage others to never give up on their recovery. I want to take care of myself. Every morning, I keep trying to fit my right shoe like

I did thousands of times in the past, which I will keep doing until the day I regain its control. Every evening, I pray that my hand will move the next day. I will keep writing about my stroke in the future. I feel content and happy when I do it.

"Don't Give in to Stroke!" This is my heartfelt message to every stroke survivor out there. No matter how challenging the journey may seem, please do not give up on yourself and your recovery. There are days when I find myself at the gym, lacking the drive to exercise, but I ask myself if there is an alternative way to train. Reminding myself that giving up on my own healing is not an option I want to pursue; I search for a different activity that engages more of my intellectual functions than physical ones. I may explore the power of visualization to aid in my progress. I envision my hand moving and tapping into the depths of my inner strength, connecting with my brain's potential to activate my finger. Today, nearly a year after the stroke, I have yet to witness visible movement in my fingers. However, in recent weeks, a glimmer of hope has emerged as I started experiencing tingling sensations in my right hand, specifically between the thumb and index. I hold onto this newfound sensation with optimism, believing it to be a promising sign that control and movement may soon return. This subtle chance fuels my perseverance, motivating me to continue with my visualization exercises and maintain hope for a brighter and more mobile future ahead. There are moments in the day when I find myself lost in daydreams, vividly envisioning myself running, writing, or driving. These mental pictures fill me with hope, a glimmer of what I aspire to achieve once more. As I immerse myself in these visions, I hold onto the belief that, one day, I will regain the ability to partake in these activities that once brought me joy and freedom.

Stroke recovery involves healing on physical, mental, and emotional levels, and it is essential to train and strengthen all three aspects. By being persistent and adaptable, we can keep pushing forward, embracing various activities that promote overall well-being and help us overcome any obstacles in our path.

"Move on, wear your stroke suit with pride." Unlike Clark Kent, I do not need a telephone booth; I wake up every morning wearing my superhero costume. I wear my stroke suit with pride, even if I limp and my hand does not move. People may stare when I walk in public spaces, but I am proud of my physical, emotional, and mental recovery journey. No one will save me, not you, nor anyone else—except ourselves. The responsibility for our own well-being and growth lies within ourselves. While support and encouragement from others can be valuable, ultimately, we hold the power to create positive change and navigate our own paths. We must take ownership of our lives, make empowering decisions, and embrace personal accountability to shape the future we desire.

Ok, perhaps someone may say that it is easy to speak in such tone for me because my deficits are not extreme like many others have. But it is not a competition to check who has disabilities or problems. We are all on this same rocky boat.

We just get in at different points. But ultimately, we are all stroke survivors. I may not have cognitive issues, except for the muscles in my mouth, which hinder my speech, but I was someone who loved running; only being able to walk like a crab doing breakdancing with curled toes is a big deal.

I am a stroke survivor, like millions of others. We are fighters. We are our own superhero. We are invincible. Each day, I tightly hold on to the two main ropes of my life: hope and faith. They guide me through challenges, providing strength and courage to face whatever comes my way. With hope in my heart and faith in the journey, I navigate life's twists and turns, knowing that brighter days lie ahead. If we cannot see the end of the tunnel, let us be the light.

In the aftermath of a stroke, success takes on a whole new meaning. No longer bound by conventional norms, we shall redefine success in a way that aligns with our post-stroke journey. It is a path characterized by resilience, self-discovery, and a commitment to consistent rehabilitation. Let us free ourselves from outdated perceptions and embrace a perspective that celebrates the small victories, hard work, and the joy of progress.

- Success after a stroke must be measured by our determination to rediscover who we are and what we love in the face of challenges.

- Consistency in rehabilitation becomes the cornerstone of success, as we embrace the journey of healing and growth, one step at a time.

- Success lies in understanding that post-stroke life is a unique and personal journey, allowing us to chart our own course and define what fulfillment means to us.
- It requires hard work, dedication, and commitment to the rehabilitation process, recognizing that each effort, no matter how small, contributes to the greater goal.
- Embrace the valuable lessons that come with stroke recovery, finding strength in the face of setbacks and rejoicing in the progress made.
- Life after stroke doesn't have to be a constant struggle; rather, it's an opportunity to savor the simplicity and joy found in the journey of recovery.
- Success is not about comparing ourselves to others but celebrating our individual growth and resilience, acknowledging that each step forward is a triumph.

In post-stroke life, success is a journey of rediscovery, consistency, and hard work. Let us release the burden of conventional measures and embrace a new perspective that cherishes progress and celebrates the resilience within. By staying committed to our rehabilitation and savoring each moment of growth, we redefine success on our terms and find fulfillment in the path we forge. Remember, the journey may be challenging, but it is also an opportunity to thrive and create a life that brings joy and purpose, post-stroke.

As I bring this book to a close, my final two cents are inscribed with heartfelt advice: "First, prioritize yourself and your recovery above all else; everything else can follow. Second, with unwavering hard work, post-stroke, one can rediscover the joy of doing what they love!" In my personal stroke recovery journey, I have found that engaging in activities I love, such as cooking, writing, and studying, has been transformative. These moments serve as major milestones, bringing joy, smiles, and inner peace to my life. As I immerse myself in these passions, I feel a sense of fulfillment and purpose, igniting a profound healing process within me. Not all superheroes wear a cape. Sometimes they wear aprons. On the same line, someone from the pizza lovers Italian Facebook group told me, “Not even a stroke can stop a pizza,” when I shared my video kneading my pizza dough.

Figure 37- Mastering Roman-Style Pizza with a Single Hand: A Culinary Triumph!

Witnessing my friends' continued appreciation for my one-handed cooking skills provides a significant morale boost. This was evident on August 6th, 2023, when I decided to take on the challenge of preparing fresh ravioli stuffed with salmon. This marked the first occasion since my stroke where I managed the entire process, from start to finish, just as I did before the stroke. The outcome, according to my friends, was exceptional—though my judgment might be influenced by personal bias. Regardless, their recognition and enjoyment of my culinary efforts serve as a reminder that my determination and adaptability continue to yield satisfying results.

***

Nearly a year has elapsed since my stroke, yet I continue to wonder if complete recovery is in my future and the potential duration of this journey. These identical inquiries often surface on the internet and within stroke survivors' groups.

It is widely understood that seeking guidance from your doctor is crucial for health concerns. Depending solely on the Internet is discouraged. Overly exaggerated information encountered online could lead to unwarranted anxiety. Conversely, if you come across information that understates your condition, you may inadvertently neglect the necessary attention it demands, potentially leading to a more critical situation.

Driven by the belief that data is inherently truthful, I delved into Google Trends to conduct research on the same subjects and queries, aiming to comprehend the typical online search patterns regarding stroke recovery.

The results show that "stroke recovery" is a popular search term and topic since 2004 in most of the countries, which is not a surprise considering that the World Stroke Organization states on their Website, "Stroke has already reached epidemic proportions. Globally 1 in 4 adults over the age of twenty-five will have a stroke in their lifetime." On the same line, the most common related searches are: "stroke recovery timeline; stroke recovery stages & exercises; stroke rehabilitation center near me; inpatient stroke rehabilitation, etc." Although I appreciate the convenience of Google Trends for swift research, I am somewhat dissatisfied with the fact that the results are not presented as absolute numbers. Instead, they present data as a ratio to the highest point on the chart for the chosen region and time.

At times, I perceive my body and essence as akin to Siamese twins—left and right sides united within one form yet bearing distinct personalities and unique perspectives on the world around them. Drawing from their unique personalities, I am crafting a new identity for myself, much like an undercover agent adapting to different roles. Or, as the popular tourist catchphrase in Thailand goes, 'Same Same, But Different.'

As I am typing the last words of this first draft, another day is finishing. Apollo, the mighty sun god, reaches the end of his arduous daily duty. The sky transforming into a canvas of vibrant colors, painted with strokes of orange, pink, and gold. The sun gracefully descends below the horizon, casting a warm, gentle glow across the desert and the sea. The world bathes in the soft embrace of twilight, as the last rays of sunlight caress the earth before bidding farewell.

I will not waste energy to worry. I will use that energy to believe. By God's grace, I will grow into the person He intended me to be. I choose to shine even after all the storm I went through. My current circumstances will not define who I am. When I am working out my right arm on the cable machine and I sense a slight pain in my shoulder area, I imagine it is the Master Puppeteer attempting to mend the broken strings. I am determined not to let the pain dominate my thoughts. I am of the belief that the stroke bestowed upon me a responsibility—to inspire and aid others in recognizing their potential and moving closer to their authentic selves. Miracles are real, and I stand as living proof. ***I am a Miracle in the Desert.***

Figure 38- Marco envisioning his path as a stroke survivor.

Stroke, a Teacher

My stroke experience felt like tough love. Though not easy to endure, it imparted valuable lessons about life. Like tough love, it challenged me to grow and learn in ways I never imagined. Despite the hardships, I have come to appreciate the profound insights and wisdom it brought into my life, making me stronger and more resilient. While the journey of recovery has its trials, I have discovered hidden strengths and newfound appreciation for life's simplest joys.

The following twelve lessons I am about to share are based on my personal experiences. The impact of a stroke can vary, and the lessons or their extent learned may differ from person to person. The lessons shared here offer insights and perspectives.

By following these tips, everyone can develop a strong sense of self and inner peace.

1) ***Remove negativity and embrace positivity in your life.*** Our lives are encircled by sources of negativity. It affects our mental and emotional states. Social media, friends, colleagues, even family. Anything and anyone can be the source of negativity. Heart breaking, but that is the reality we live in. Surrounding yourself with positivity is one step closer to living your best life. Browsing social media or reading the news can put you into a negative mental state. Thus, reduce

the time spent doing those activities. Instead, do things that you find rejuvenating or constructive. One of your family members or friends is pulling you into their sphere of negative energy. Choose to spend time with more positive people instead. A stroke can shift one's perspective on life, priorities, and what matters.

2) ***Stop worrying about things you can never ever control.*** Looking back is not about dwelling in the past. It is a tool for personal growth and understanding. Embrace the memories, learn from them. Appreciate the journey that has led you to where you are today and use the learnt lessons to make a better future. Regrets are a waste of time. “The more you're afraid to fail, the more likely you are to fail!!” and “The more you fail, the more likely you are to succeed!!!!”

3) ***Reframe thoughts to find a positive perspective.*** Reframing requires seeing something in a new way. In a context that allows us to appreciate the positive aspects of our new situation. Reframing helps us to use whatever life hands us as opportunities. They are advantages rather than problems. Reframing is not a denial that the challenges we are currently dealing with are difficult ones. I keep telling myself, “I need to keep writing to finish this book,” although it is time and energy consuming. A positive mindset is a great way to change perspective and improve mental health. You can learn to cultivate mindfulness by focusing on

the present and finding gratitude for small victories and everyday joys.

4) ***Recite a positive inner monologue.*** A person's inner dialogue is mostly made of adverse self-talk. Most of the time, it comprises negative things about ourselves, negative emotions, or us trying to decide if we are good enough. Creating a positive inner voice brings many advantages. It is a window to a better you and a better life. It is one of the biggest investments you can make in yourself. Engage yourself in a daily routine reminding yourself to have only positive thoughts. Your confidence will increase, and you will feel happier. You can even write and recite a longer positive affirmation each morning. This has been proven to improve mental health. In life, the way we perceive and experience our reality is profoundly influenced by the words we speak to ourselves. Every day, I make it a point to practice positive self-talk, and the experience has been truly energizing and fulfilling. By consciously choosing words of encouragement, self-compassion, and optimism, I have noticed a significant shift in my mindset and overall outlook on life.

6) ***Take care of your body***. Your mental welfare is strongly linked to your physical well-being. It is much easier to maintain a cheerful outlook when you get enough sleep, drink enough water, and exercise regularly. Simple changes like getting eight hours of

sleep a night or going for a walk every day might be the key to finding that new perspective and sustaining a positive outlook. Additionally, learn how to manage and reduce stress, and seek appropriate medical care. Incorporating mindfulness practices, such as meditation or deep breathing exercises, can help you develop self-awareness and manage stress.

7) ***Perform charitable deeds.*** When you do a good deed for others, you will transform their day to a better one. Studies show that doing something pleasant for someone else can make your day a little better too. It can be as little as greeting strangers on the road with a smile. Give some cash to the less fortunate.

8) ***Write down everything that is in your mind and heart.*** When you write your thoughts down, something takes over and the writing becomes more serious and more purposeful. It is like magic. In a short while, the mind calms down and reorganizes. It is probably because in the process of writing, feelings and emotions become clearer and hidden thoughts and feelings come to the surface to bring a more complete light to the situation. In time, what is really bothering you, what has been obscured by incessant worrying and obsessive repetition of the same thoughts, comes to the surface as clear as daylight. It is extremely satisfying when writing down your thoughts and feelings results in insights into yourself, other people, and situations.

You grow in personal wisdom that can serve you, and others, for the rest of your life, and that is very fulfilling. You become an asset to society because you are growing in self-awareness.

9) ***Embrace a personal spiritual practice.*** Cultivate a personal spiritual practice that aligns with your beliefs and resonates with you. This may involve prayer, meditation, gratitude practices, or any other form of connecting with the divine or higher power. Regularly engaging in a personal spiritual practice can deepen your connection and sense of faith. Your faith will get you through these tough times to reach your future.

10) ***Seek guidance and support.*** The more honest you are about your faults and struggles; the more people will think you are perfect. The amazing thing about vulnerability is the more comfortable you are about not being that great, the more people will think you are. The support of family, friends, and caregivers plays a vital role in the recovery process. Stroke survivors realize the importance of surrounding themselves with a staunch support system that can provide encouragement, understanding, and assistance. If you are struggling with questions or doubts, consider seeking guidance from religious leaders, spiritual teachers, or counselors who can provide insights and support. They can help address your concerns, clarify your beliefs, and guide you on your path.

11) ***Explore new abilities:*** While a stroke may have caused certain limitations, it can also uncover previously untapped strengths and abilities. As you undergo rehabilitation, you may discover new talents, interests, or ways of thinking that can become integral parts of your post-stroke identity.

All the above lessons can be summarized with the most important one:

12) ***Become Unfuckwithable.*** It requires obtaining an intense sense of self-worth and inner peace that is not shaken by what others say or do. Here are some tips to reach that state of mind:

    a. Understand who you are and what you believe in.

    b. Learn from mistakes and focus on getting better.

    c. Look after your physical and mental health by doing things you enjoy.

    d. See challenges as opportunities to grow and become stronger.

    e. Surround yourself with people who lift you up and avoid negative influences.

    f. Focus on things you can change and accept what you cannot.

    g. Appreciate the good things in your life and focus on what you have.

h. Have confidence in your abilities and trust your instincts.

i. Becoming "Unfuckwithable" takes time and effort, but it is worth it.

j. Sometimes, you just have to say “F*ck You” to all the cynics and pessimists and live your life the way you choose.

Letter To My Stroke

Dear Stroke,

As our first anniversary approaches, or I shall say strokiversary, I find myself reflecting on the journey we have shared, marked by highs, and lows, struggles, and triumphs. You were the unexpected guest in my life, and our relationship has been nothing short of complex. In many ways, you brought me to the lowest points I have ever experienced. There were moments when you felt like an anchor, dragging me down as I fought to keep my head above water.

But amidst the struggle to stay afloat, something profound occurred. You became a teacher in disguise, a relentless challenge that pushed me to learn about myself and the essence of life itself. At times, you were like a magnifying glass, amplifying my imperfections and limitations. With your lens focused sharply, I had to confront aspects of myself that I had long avoided. You made me fully aware of my body and the intricate connection between body and mind.

You have taught me more about life and myself than I had learned in 30 years of reading and studying before you entered my life with such an impact.

Drawing inspiration from my Hindu friends, the red dots adorning their foreheads, you have opened my third eye, a concept often referred to as the mind's eye or inner eye. In Hinduism, the term "third eye" pertains to the ajna (or brow) chakra. According to Hindu tradition, everyone possesses a third inner eye. The two physical eyes perceive the external world, while the third directs its gaze inward, toward the divine.

You forced me to see my life from an entirely different perspective. Through your presence, I gained a microscope to examine my flaws and insecurities, magnified a hundredfold. I could no longer ignore these aspects; I had to confront them head-on. You functioned as a catalyst for self-awareness, revealing layers of myself that were previously hidden.

It is fascinating how you opened my eyes to a world I had overlooked. In that pivotal moment, you were not aiming to destroy me; instead, you were saving me from the path of self-neglect. You illuminated a new way of living, one that is richer in meaning and purpose. You showed me that life is not to be taken for granted, and that each moment holds significance.

Though you presented immense challenges, you gifted me with newfound purposes. You encouraged me to reshape my priorities, to prioritize health, happiness, and the pursuit of genuine fulfillment. It was through your presence that I realized the fragility of existence and the urgency to make the most of it.

You have shown me that every day is a canvas for beauty, regardless of the adversity life presents. Life is beautiful even after a stroke.

How do I manage to see life as beautiful even after a stroke? This question has been posed to me multiple times over the past months. My approach is not rooted in magic or novelty; it is a simple recipe that keeps me motivated and content:

**Daily Gratitude: ** Every day, I express gratitude to God for granting me another day and for sparing me during that fateful moment. He had no intention of letting me perish in the desert.

**Positive Self-Talk: ** Daily self-talk is my tonic—I remind myself of my strength, my survivor spirit, my miraculous journey, and my status as a superhero donning an apron instead of a cape. I passionately believe that I can accomplish anything if I put in the effort.

**Pursuit of Joy: ** I channel my energy into activities that fill me with joy: cooking, learning, writing, and cherishing time with family and friends.

**Setting Goals: ** Long-term goals anchor me. My aims are reclaiming the use of my right hand and resuming running. Given their scope, I have subdivided them into smaller milestones, like slicing a pizza for manageable bites. Celebrating each small victory and not lamenting setbacks fuels my determination.

**Acceptance and Adaptation: ** I am grateful for the functionalities I have regained, but I've also made peace with the fact that if I do not achieve my long-term aspirations, I'll be okay. Life will persist, and I will uncover fresh objectives and purposes. I have honed skills like cooking and crafting a book with my left hand alone.

**Work-Life Balance: ** Balancing work and personal life is pivotal. Recognizing that stress, whether work-induced or self-imposed, could have contributed to my stroke, I have realigned my priorities, putting my health before my job, despite my affection for it.

**Positive Social Circle: ** I surround myself solely with positive influences—people who contribute positivity. Negative individuals are kept at arm's length.

**Self-Care First: ** For me, my own well-being takes precedence; others and everything else come second.

**Embrace Forgiveness and Release the Past: ** I cultivate forgiveness towards myself, letting go of past mistakes and regrets. I embrace the present moment as a chance for growth and renewal.

**Cultivate Self-Confidence, Self-Belief, and Purpose: ** I nurture a strong sense of self-assurance, recognizing my worth and capabilities in the face of adversity. I foster a deep belief in my potential to triumph over obstacles and shape my own destiny. I discover and embrace my new life's purpose, recognizing that every experience, including challenges like a stroke, can contribute to my unique journey.

So, as we mark this anniversary, I cannot deny the transformation you have brought into my life. Our relationship has been a paradox—filled with struggle yet leading to growth. You have changed the trajectory of my story, steering it towards self-discovery, resilience, and embracing the extraordinary beauty of life's intricate details.

Stroke, I find myself incredibly proud of the person you have molded me into over this past year.

With gratitude for the lessons learned and the strength gained,

Marco

Conclusion

"Don't quit. Suffer now and live the rest of your life as a champion." - Muhammad Ali.

My take on this quote, in the context of stroke recovery is to persist through the struggles of stroke recovery, for it paves the path to championing life. Embrace challenges, never quit, and find strength in the journey. Each step forward leads to triumph, shaping a resilient and victorious future.

Yes, it was a distressing accident which paved the way to a long recovery which is still ongoing. But besides pain and destress, there was growth, a lot of it in fact. It is common that people who have survived trauma find positive changes as well. New appreciation for life. A new sense of personal strength and a new focus on helping others. My memoir has been a journey of self-discovery, resilience, and growth. I came out of it changed, victorious, with a new perspective. It is a testament to the power of the human spirit. The ability to overcome obstacles and achieve personal transformation. I worked on myself by moving a step forward every day. I stayed committed and focused. I was able to walk away from the edge of depression.

By sharing my experience, I hope to inspire others to embrace their own unique journeys. To find strength in their vulnerabilities. To never underestimate the power of perseverance. Life is a series of chapters, each one filled with lessons and opportunities for growth. As I close this memoir, I am grateful for the experiences that have shaped me and the people who have touched my life. I leave you with the idea that our stories are not just meant to be written—they are meant to be lived, cherished, and shared. Through sharing our stories, we connect with others and leave an indelible mark on the world. I encourage you to embark on your own remarkable journey of self-discovery.

In the Odysseus, Ulysses finished his journey back home in Itaca. Likewise, these are the last words of my hero's journey. So, with a heart full of gratitude and a mind eager for the next chapter, I bid you farewell. Paraphrasing the great Toto in "Miseria e Nobilta," I say: "It is enough for me to know that the public is happy reading this book, like I was writing it."

"Whispers of Courage"

In a world of uncertainty, a stroke did unfold,
A sudden interruption, a story yet untold.
A tempest in the mind, a storm within the soul,
Yet through the darkest hours, strength begins to grow.

Like a whisper in the wind, life took an unexpected turn,
But within this new journey, there is much we can learn.
With each step forward, resilience finds its way,
A spirit undeterred, finding hope in every day.

In the realm of rehabilitation, battles are fought,
Reclaiming independence, each victory sought.
A symphony of courage, as hearts and minds align,
To rebuild what was shattered, to defy the confines.

Through therapies and patience, progress takes its place,
Healing becomes a dance, grace bestowed with grace.
The road may be winding, but determination prevails,
Embracing newfound strength, as resilience never fails.

With love and support, a community stands strong,
Together we rise, where belonging does belong.
In the face of adversity, we find the will to cope,
For within the stroke's embrace, we discover newfound hope.

Bibliography

Anxiety disorders - Symptoms and causes - Mayo Clinic (2018). Available at: https://www.mayoclinic.org/diseases-conditions/anxiety/symptoms-causes/syc-20350961.

BA, C.L. (2020) "What Is Synchronicity and How to Recognize the Signs of It in Your Life - Learning Mind," *Learning Mind* [Preprint]. Available at: https://www.learning-mind.com/what-is-synchronicity/.

Bear, B. (2020) "“ Everything in Life is Temporary” 5 Life Lessons," *Brightside Bear* [Preprint]. Available at: https://brightsidebear.com/everything-temporary-quote/.

Bloom, S. and Bloom, S. (2012) "Why It's Hard to Do Things That Are Good for You," *Do Something Cool | Get More Out of Life* [Preprint]. Available at: http://dosomethingcool.net/why-hard-things-good/.

Botox injections - Mayo Clinic (2023). Available at: https://www.mayoclinic.org/tests-procedures/botox/about/pac-20384658.

BSc, L.R. (2020) "How Your Intuition Reveals Your Brain's Best Decisions - Learning Mind," *Learning Mind* [Preprint].

Available at: https://www.learning-mind.com/how-your-intuition-reveals-your-brains-best-decisions/.

Burns, H. (2023a) "5 Habits of Unsuccessful People: Rich vs. Poor Mindset - New Trader U," *New Trader U*, 28 May. Available at: https://www.newtraderu.com/2023/05/28/5-habits-of-unsuccessful-people-rich-vs-poor-mindset/.

Burns, H. (2023b) "How To Be Unshakeable in Every Situation (Stoic Life Lessons Quotes) - New Trader U," *New Trader U*, 9 June. Available at: https://www.newtraderu.com/2023/05/21/how-to-be-unshakeable-in-every-situation-stoic-life-lessons-quotes/.

Burns, H. (2023c) *if(typeof ez_ad_units!='undefined'){ez_ad_units.push([[728,90],'newtraderu_com-box-2','ezslot_11',610,'0']});__ez_fad_position('div-gpt-ad-newtraderu_com-box-2-0');20 Great Habits For A Positive Mental Attitude – Napoleon Hill*. Available at: https://www.newtraderu.com/2023/06/23/20-great-habits-for-a-positive-mental-attitude-napoleon-hill/.

Camus, Albert | Internet Encyclopedia of Philosophy (no date). Available at: https://iep.utm.edu/albert-camus/.

Carson, R. (1983) *Taming Your Gremlin*. HarpPeren.

Choosing Therapy (2023) "Defensive Pessimism: Definition & Effectiveness," *Choosing Therapy* [Preprint]. Available at: https://www.choosingtherapy.com/defensive-pessimism/.

Cline, A. (2019) "Karl Marx on Religion as the Opium of the

People," *Learn Religions* [Preprint]. Available at: https://www.learnreligions.com/karl-marx-on-religion-251019.

Crimmins, C. (2001) *Where Is the Mango Princess? A Journey Back From Brain Injury*. National Geographic Books.

Dahlgren, K. (2016) *Healing and Happiness After Stroke: How to Get Back Up After Life Turned Upside-Down.*

Dennis, N. (2023a) "Who am I"; The answer to life's most defining question," *Ideapod*, 28 May. Available at: https://ideapod.com/who-am-i-the-answer-to-lifes-most-defining-question/#:~:text=The%20%E2%80%9Canswer%E2%80%9D%20to%20%E2%80%9Cwho%20am%20I%E2%80%9D%20is%20our,a%20critical%20component%20of%20understanding%20who%20we%20are.

Depression (major depressive disorder) - Symptoms and causes - Mayo Clinic (2022). Available at: https://www.mayoclinic.org/diseases-conditions/depression/symptoms-causes/syc-20356007.

Dixon, J.K. and Dixon, J. (2013) *A Stroke of Luck: A Girl's Second Chance at Life.*

Faulkner, H. (2023) *Faith Still Moves Mountains: Miraculous Stories of the Healing Power of Prayer.* Broadside Books.

Forgeard, V. (2022) "Is Positive Mindset a Skill (Answered) - brilliantio," *brilliantio*, 17 February.

Available at: https://brilliantio.com/is-positive-mindset-a-skill/#:~:text=Related%20Articles-,A%20Positive%20Mindset%20Is%20Everything,your%20career%20and%20your%20life.

Gill, N.S. (2019) "Ulysses (Odysseus)," *ThoughtCo* [Preprint]. Available at: https://www.thoughtco.com/who-is-ulysses-homers-odyssey-119101.

Hazelton, C. *et al.* (2022) "Perceptual Disorders After Stroke: A Scoping Review of Interventions," *Stroke*, 53(5), pp. 1772–1787. Available at: https://doi.org/10.1161/strokeaha.121.035671.

Holiday, R. (2017) "What Is Memento Mori?" *Daily Stoic* [Preprint]. Available at: https://dailystoic.com/what-is-memento-mori/.

Home - Recovery After Stroke (2021). Available at: https://recoveryafterstroke.com/.

How Values Shape Identity (2023). Available at: https://values.institute/how-values-shape-identity/.

Ischemic Stroke (Clots) (no date). Available at: https://www.stroke.org/en/about-stroke/types-of-stroke/ischemic-stroke-clots.

Johnson, J.M. (2014) "There Is No Such Thing as a Coincidence," *HuffPost UK*, 1 April. Available at: https://www.huffingtonpost.co.uk/jessica-mcgregor-johnson/coincidence_b_4695324.html.

Karr, M. (2016) *The Art of Memoir*. Harper Perennial.

Laurence, E. and Laurence, E. (2021) "This Is the Secret to Recognizing Serendipity—and How To Use It in Your Life," *Well+Good* [Preprint]. Available at: https://www.wellandgood.com/what-is-serendipity/.

Libretexts (2023) "9.17: Erikson - Integrity vs. Despair," *Social Sci LibreTexts* [Preprint]. Available at: https://socialsci.libretexts.org/Bookshelves/Psychology/Developmental_Psychology/Lifespan_Development_-_A_Psychological_Perspective_(Lally_and_Valentine-French)/09%3A_Late_Adulthood/9.17%3A_Erikson_-_Integrity_vs._Despair#:~:text=It%20is%20also%20feeling%20a%20sense%20of%20contentment,one%20to%20despair%20at%20the%20end%20of%20life.

Marcus Aurelius (Stanford Encyclopedia of Philosophy) (2017). Available at: https://plato.stanford.edu/entries/marcus-aurelius/.

Margaret (2021) "Taming Your Inner Demons. The Role Of Shame: One Question That Helps," *Dr. Margaret Rutherford* [Preprint]. Available at: https://drmargaretrutherford.com/taming-your-inner-demons-the-role-of-shame-in-perfectly-hidden-depression/.

McCall, R. (2019) "The Human Body Is 99 Percent Empty Space - So Why Can't We Walk Through Walls?" *IFLScience* [Preprint]. Available at: https://www.iflscience.com/the-human-body-is-99-percent-empty-space-so-why-cant-we-walk-through-walls-47375.

Miglani, B. (2021) *4 Reasons to Stop Worrying About*

the Future. Available at: https://embracethechaos.com/2012/07/4-reasons-to-stop-worrying-about-the-future/.

MSEd, K.C. (2022) "What Is Cognitive Dissonance?" *Verywell Mind* [Preprint]. Available at: https://www.verywellmind.com/what-is-cognitive-dissonance-2795012.

MSEd, K.C. (2023) "Catharsis in Psychology," *Verywell Mind* [Preprint]. Available at: https://www.verywellmind.com/what-is-catharsis-2794968.

Nathan, L. (2023) "Improve brain power for study, work and focus: Everything you need to know," *Study International* [Preprint]. Available at: https://www.studyinternational.com/news/improve-brain-power-study-focus/.

Oppong, T. (2022) "The Pragmatic Optimist: A Practical Way to Think About Your Future," *Medium*, 15 February. Available at: https://betterhumans.pub/the-pragmatic-optimist-a-practical-way-to-think-about-your-future-b48afa13de9d.

Orlando Neuro Therapy (2022) *Stroke Physical Therapy | Move BETTER and IMPROVE YOUR LIFE!* Available at: https://orlandoneurotherapy.com/stroke/.

Otr/L, C.M. (2022) "Stroke Recovery Timeline: How Long Does It Take to Recover?" *Flint Rehab* [Preprint]. Available at: https://www.flintrehab.com/stroke-recovery-timeline/.

Pasricha, N. (2023) "I've written 10 books on happiness—here are 5 tiny habits that make me feel happier and healthier every day," *CNBC*, 22 June. Available at: https://www.cnbc.com/2023/06/22/ive-written-10-books-about-happiness-here-are-science-backed-habits-i-do-every-day-to-feel-happier.html.

Prati, M. (2022) "Self-irony. Chaplin's secret to not taking yourself too seriously," *Medium*, 5 February. Available at: https://medium.com/@mariopratizy/self-irony-chaplins-secret-to-not-taking-yourself-too-seriously-40e174ef1fe1#:~:text=Self%2Dirony%20is%20the%20ability,up%20taking%20themselves%20too%20seriously.

Priya, R. (2014) *Sociology of Religion: Max Weber*. Available at: https://www.yourarticlelibrary.com/sociology/sociology-of-religion-max-weber/43751.

Professional, C.C.M. (no date a) *Foot Drop*. Available at: https://my.clevelandclinic.org/health/diseases/17814-foot-drop.

Professional, C.C.M. (no date b) *Spasticity*. Available at: https://my.clevelandclinic.org/health/diseases/14346-spasticity.

Professional, C.C.M. (no date c) *Thrombectomy*. Available at: https://my.clevelandclinic.org/health/treatments/22897-thrombectomy.

Pseudobulbar affect - Symptoms and causes - Mayo Clinic (2018). Available at: https://www.mayoclinic.org/diseases-conditions/pseudobulbar-affect/symptoms-causes/syc-20353737#:~:text=Pseudobulbar%20affect%20(PBA)%20 is%20a,way%20the%20brain%20controls%20emotion.

Richard (2022) "How to answer “ who am I? ”" *Life After the Daily Grind* [Preprint]. Available at: https://lifeafterthedailygrind.com/how-to-answer-who-am-i/.

Rogers, M. (2022) *A Stroke of Heaven: Processing a Brain Injury and the Events Thereafter Through a Spiritual Lens.* WestBow Press.

Saebo (2022) *Stroke Rehabilitation Exercises for Your Entire Body | Saebo, Inc.* Available at: https://www.saebo.com/stroke-exercises-for-your-body/.

Scott, E., PhD (2022) "Signs of Pessimism and How to Respond," *Verywell Mind* [Preprint]. Available at: https://www.verywellmind.com/is-it-safer-to-be-a-pessimist-3144874.

Should I kill myself or have a cup of coffee? (2023). Available at: https://iai.tv/articles/should-i-kill-myself-or-have-a-cup-of-coffee-the-stoics-and-existentialists-agree-on-the-answer-auid-924.

Simply Sociology (2023) *Karl Marx on Religion: Ideas & Quotes.* Available at: https://simplysociology.com/karl-marx-on-religion.html.

Slater, B. (2023) "Start with Clarity and Brevity (But Don' t Forget the Context, Impact And Value) - The Latimer Group," *The Latimer Group*, 26 January. Available at: https://thelatimergroup.com/start-with-clarity-

and-brevity-and-dont-forget-the-context-impact-and-value/#:~:text=Clarity%2C%20for%20example%2C%20ensures%20that,saturated%2C%20data%2Dintensive%20world.

Stroke - Symptoms and causes - Mayo Clinic (2023). Available at: https://www.mayoclinic.org/diseases-conditions/stroke/symptoms-causes/syc-20350113.

Stroke Recovery Timeline (2022). Available at: https://www.hopkinsmedicine.org/health/conditions-and-diseases/stroke/stroke-recovery-timeline.

Summers, J. (2023) *if(typeof ez_ad_units!='undefined'){ez_ad_units.push([[728,90],'newtraderu_com-box-2','ezslot_9',610,'0','0']};__ez_fad_position('div-gpt-ad-newtraderu_com-box-2-0');Three Keys To Achieve Anything In Life*. Available at: https://www.newtraderu.com/2023/06/23/three-keys-to-achieve-anything-in-life/.

Taylor, J.B. (2009) *My Stroke of Insight: A Brain Scientist's Personal Journey*. Plume Books.

The Apostle Paul's Secret to Contentment (no date). Available at: https://www.crossway.org/articles/the-secret-of-contentment-challies/.

The Editors of Encyclopaedia Britannica (2023) *The Divine Comedy | Dante, Poem, Summary, & Facts*. Available at: https://www.britannica.com/topic/The-Divine-Comedy.

Thestyledseed (2018) *The Art of Celebrating Everything and Nothing; Simplicity, Gratitude & More*. Available at: https://www.delaneychilds.com/celebrate-nothing-celebrate-everything-simplicity-gratitude-and-spontaneity/.

Ulysses and the Sirens (no date). Available at: https://www.historytoday.com/archive/foundations/ulysses-and-sirens.

Vedantu (no date) "The Chinese Bamboo Story - Learn Powerful Life Lessons," *VEDANTU* [Preprint]. Available at: https://www.vedantu.com/stories/chinese-bamboo-tree-story.

Villines, Z. (2023) *What to know about inappropriate laughter*. Available at: https://www.medicalnewstoday.com/articles/inappropriate-laughter#definition.

Volenik, A. (2023) "12 things to remember when you're feeling stuck in life," *Hack Spirit* [Preprint]. Available at: https://hackspirit.com/things-to-remember-when-youre-feeling-stuck-in-life/.

Walia, N. (2018) "Celebrate Everything!" *The Times of India*, 19 October. Available at: https://timesofindia.indiatimes.com/life-style/health-fitness/de-stress/celebrate-everything/articleshow/66272611.cms.

Weaver, T. (2023) "Stoic Belief - The Philosophy Of Virtue And Ethics," *Orion Philosophy* [Preprint]. Available at: https://www.orionphilosophy.com/stoic-blog/stoicism-beliefs#:~:text=%E2%80%9CPhilosophy%20does%20not%20promise%20to,is%20each%20person%27s%20own%20life.%E2%80%9D.

Weidmann, J. (no date) *The Power of Contentment:*

Three Ways to Change Your Perspective Quickly | Josh Weidmann. Available at: https://joshweidmann.com/the-power-of-contentment/.

What Is Defensive Pessimism, And Is It Healthy? | BetterHelp (no date). Available at: https://www.betterhelp.com/advice/pessimism/what-is-defensive-pessimism-and-is-it-healthy/.

Why Should You Write Your Memoir? (no date). Available at: https://www.psychologytoday.com/intl/blog/the-empowerment-diary/201609/why-should-you-write-your-memoir.

Wiest, B. (2014) *How To Tame Your Inner Demons*. Available at: https://thoughtcatalog.com/brianna-wiest/2014/04/how-to-tame-your-inner-demons/.

Wikipedia contributors (2023) "Paradiso (Dante)," *Wikipedia* [Preprint]. Available at: https://en.wikipedia.org/wiki/Paradiso_(Dante).

雨燕体育(科技)有限公司 - 百度百科 (no date). Available at: https://www.provita-me.com/.

About the Author

Marco Giovannoli was born in 1976 and raised in the gentle hills outside Rome, Italy. Since he was a child, he has always enjoyed penning down his thoughts. He is a successful Aeronautical Engineer living in Abu Dhabi, United Arab Emirates. He was an active runner until that day in September 2022 when he suffered a life-altering stroke while running, which turned his world upside down. Marco found inner strength, renewed faith, and a new sensc of purpose after the stroke, becoming a "Miracle in the Desert."

Curious about Marco's inspiring journey? Follow his progress on his Facebook profile "Marco Gio" at https://www.facebook.com/profile.php?id=100092988341519&mibextid=9R9pXO

Or send him an email at m.giovannoli1@gmail.com

www.ingramcontent.com/pod-product-compliance
Lightning Source LLC
LaVergne TN
LVHW010051170826
845678LV00012B/2107

* 9 7 8 8 1 1 9 2 2 3 8 8 6 *